LAUGHTER AND TEARS

LAUGHTER AND TEARS

Margery McDowall

LAUGHTER AND TEARS
ISBN 1 901 442 21 7

Typeset in Sabon by Kestrel Data, Exeter, Devon.

Printed in Great Britain by Short Run Press Limited, Exeter, Devon.

*To my three children, Colin, David and Sandra,
and my son-in-law Steve, without whose help
this book may never have been written.*

CONTENTS

CHAPTER ONE

1918

IN THE BEGINNING

The fog was already descending and the maroons could be heard in the distance across the River Mersey. It was a dismal, cold February evening and one which will be etched in my memory forever.

We had been visiting my aunt. I always enjoyed going as there was so much to see: lots of shining brasses and a parrot in a big cage, which kept chunnering to itself and would then suddenly, in a loud voice shout "Echo and Express!" I used to be a bit afraid when my uncle let it out of the cage but it would just fly to him and sit on his shoulder. After we had had tea, Auntie would reach up to the high mantelpiece and bring down a tin box, her "trick box" as she called it. For me it was the peak of my visit.

I loved that box. There was always such exciting things in it: coloured marbles, buttons of all shapes and sizes, chalks, pencils, rings and lots of novelties from Christmas crackers. There was always something new. When Mum said it was time to go home, I parted with it very reluctantly.

"Never mind," said Auntie, "next time, there'll be even more treasures in it." That trick box lasted many years and kept many a child happy.

It was about ten o'clock when we left for home and made the long walk to the tram stop. I was only five years old and my little legs felt tired. I held Mum's hand and Dad carried my new baby sister who was just two months old. When the tram-car arrived it was quite full, but Mum sat on one side between two ladies, with the baby on her knees. I sat on my father's knee, but on the other side, near the driver. The motion of the tram was sending me to sleep when my dad spoke in my ear.

"Come on, you mustn't go to sleep, we are getting off next stop". At that moment the trolley came off the overhead cable and the tram-car was plunged into darkness. Outside a thick fog had now developed and I couldn't see a thing out of the window. Then it happened. A terrific bang, people screaming, glass shattering. I'll never forget it.

"Daddy! Daddy! Is the baby all right?"

People surrounded Mum. Dad was very calm and guided everybody off by the driver's door. Mother and Baby were both all right, which was very lucky; all the windows were broken where they had been sitting. We were only five minutes from home, so we were soon safe and sound. Years later, my dad told me that a motor car had crashed into the stationary tram and had killed an old lady. The driver of the car had also been very badly injured.

*   *   *

I always thought what a grand sounding name our road, Burleigh Road North had. It stands today pretty much as it did eighty-three years ago when I was born in house number eight, except that the lovely old church of St Cuthbert which stood at the top of the road has gone and houses have been built in its place.

The road is unique, for although they were terraced houses, they were not all the same. All had bay windows and our house had a small garden frontage of about 1½ yards with a hedge. Further down the road, the paths and gardens were very much longer. Across the road, all the houses had long pathways and bigger gardens but every house still only had a back yard with doors opening out into a long narrow entry.

Many people came down the entry selling goods. One old lady used to carry large slabs of salt on her head. When Mum heard her deep voice shouting "Salt!" she would hurry out to buy some off her. Later, Lol and I would have the job of cutting and crushing it and putting it into containers or jars. Another cry "Lemons! any lemons?". Another was "Any, any old jars?" Lol and I would ask Mum if she had any and out we would go. For six jars we got 3d and for one jar, a balloon. "Any old clothes?", was another cry. Oh! our entry was always very busy.

We were not bothered much with front-door sellers but when the syrup man came around, Mum always got some lovely raw golden syrup. The man would ladle it out of a big container and it was great on our "butties". The "Aunt Sally" man came every fortnight, selling disinfectant and soft soap.

I loved my home. It had no bathroom, but every Saturday night, Lol and I were bathed in a tin bath in front of the fire. After our bath we knelt by my Mum's knee and had our hair combed through with a fine-toothed comb. She did this regularly to keep us from getting head lice. After that we had a weekly dose of Syrup of Senna. I hated it. I didn't like the smell of it and used to hold my nose.

We had our meals in the kitchen which was graced with a black iron fireplace with a hob. On it stood a big iron kettle from which we got any hot water we needed. Each week the whole range had to be back-leaded. It was an awesome job but after Mum's hard work it was bright and shining. Our back kitchen had a round brick boiler with a small fire underneath, which Mum used to light on washing day. It would fill with water to boil the clothes. After the washing was done, the water was used to wash the outside toilet, scrub the table and swill the backyard and that was the end of washing day. It lasted all day and was always on a Monday.

Mum's friend, Mrs Davis, lived opposite to us. She was a good-looking woman but was slightly deaf. She very kindly said Lol and I could go to her house after school to listen to *Children's Hour* on the radio. When we arrived, Lol and I were handed heavy headphones to put on. They were so big we had to hold them up over our ears and it was always so loud. We hated going but she thought that she was doing us a good turn. We weren't rich enough to have a radio.

If anyone died in our road it was a recognised thing that Mrs Davis and Mum would lay them out ready for burial. A funeral in those days was a very special, spectacular affair. A beautiful glass hearse drawn by black horses would arrive. If the funeral was for a child then the horses would wear white ribbons. If it was for an adult then black ribbons would be worn. There was always plenty of lovely flowers, no matter how poor the circumstances. The kind neighbours would see to that and dig deep in their pockets giving as much as they could afford.

Four houses down the road from Mrs Davis lived a Mrs Bogle. She was a dear old soul. She lived on her own but had a little black dog. Every now and again the poor thing had a big bandage tied around its bottom. Being very innocent, we asked her what was the matter. She would just glare at us and hurry into the house. It was many years later before we realised what a dog in season meant!

Burleigh Road had its share of tragedy. My best friend Grace, who went to school with me, lost her mother who had been very ill for some time. After she died, Grace's father just couldn't take her loss and one morning he hanged himself at work. We all felt so very sad.

Three doors from where Grace lived a widow lady resided with her two little daughters. She used to go out early as she was a cleaner. The girls aged eight and six used to get themselves off to school.

"I wish you wouldn't go out, Mum," the eldest Edna, said one day. Her mother asked her why. "As soon as you've gone," she replied. "Gwladys and I have to go to bed with the lodger." The police came and took him away. I don't know what happened to him.

On a Saturday, Lol and I always got a penny from Mum. I would also scrub the lady next-door's steps and she would give me a penny. So with our *twopences* there was great speculation on how we would spend our wealth. We decided to join a Christmas club at a draper's shop. We did this, saving *twopence* a week all year so that we could buy Mum and Dad a present at Christmas. We got so much pleasure out of doing this.

Our parlour had a piano in it which belonged to my grandmother who was a music teacher. For two years I used to have lessons. I liked my nana a lot but she had a rather long, beaky nose and there always seemed to be a large dewdrop on the end of it. It fascinated me, but when I was doing scales, I was scared it would drop onto my hand. In the end, I had to speak to her.

"Your nose wants wiping." For my pains I got a swipe on my knuckles with the ruler that she always carried.

"Get on with your music!" was her reply.

One summer, when I was about twelve, I collected about ten frogs and Dad got me a big tea chest to keep them in. I lined the bottom with grass sods and kept them in the backyard, feeding them on big garden worms. My friends in the road kept coming to the house with worms for "Margery's frogs". Mum used to get fed up answering the door all the time. Very often, I would fill the tin bath with water to give them a swim. They became so very tame. I really loved them. I used to hold out my hand and they would jump on it. I kept those frogs for nearly four months. Then, one tragic day, I came home from school, ran into the yard to see my little pets. They had gone!

"Mum, where are my frogs?" I cried, running into the kitchen.

Mum told me that she had flushed them down the toilet. She said winter was coming on and she thought it was the best thing to do. She said that they wouldn't die, just swim away. I was broken-hearted. I loved them so much.

My mum and dad were the best and kindest parents any child could wish for. They never drank and I never even heard either of them swear. We were strictly brought up with a very religious background. We went to church three times on a Sunday and, as if that wasn't enough, after evening service an old decripid organ was rolled along the road and we had an outside service where we stood around singing hymns, hoping passers-by would join in. I also belonged to St Mary's Girl Guides, who were the 1st Liverpool Company. I enjoyed that very much.

One Christmas, Lol and I got a lovely doll each from Mum and Dad. They had china faces, eyes with long eyelashes and lovely hair with ringlets. We loved those dolls. We were only allowed to play with them on a Sunday and on special occasions. After having them a few years, Mother asked Lol and I if we would make a sacrifice and give our dolls to the church to be raffled, the proceeds going to the church funds. I couldn't believe it! Our lovely dolls! They were the best present we had ever been given. I handed my lovely doll to Mum and in the quiet of my bedroom I shed many a silent tear.

Sometimes on a Saturday, Lol and I would hold a one penny bazaar in the backyard. We had a stall and would put some little things that we had made on a bench: knick-knacks, marbles and dolls clothes. When we had sold out, we spent the money on lemonade powder and biscuits etc. Mum would make our drinks and all the children who had come to buy, joined in the party.

*   *   *

My dad had two sisters, Clara and Gertie, and they married two brothers, Bridger and William Barton. Auntie Gertie was of a rather quiet disposition but I thought that she was quite beautiful. About twelve months after she and Willie married she had a little baby daughter, Betty. She was a very cross baby, always crying. When Betty was two my auntie found that she was expecting again and Uncle Willie laughed. "If it's another girl," he said, "I'll drown it!"

Well, it was another little girl but she only lived for three weeks. Auntie couldn't get over the baby's death. She blamed Willie because of what he had said. She brooded and wouldn't go out, staying in bed all day. She started to have a mental breakdown and in the end, was taken to Whittingham Asylum and died there many years later.

Auntie Clara had three children, Cecil, Joyce and Harry. She was a very versatile person. She could sing, play the piano and sew. She was always sewing. I remember her making me a blue velvet dress with white swans down around the neck and sleeves. The feathers kept getting in the mouth all the time and I didn't like it at all. I felt like a duck! She even used to make hats out of crepe paper but they were very good. She would cut the cream paper into strips, plait it and make the crown of the hat by sewing the plaits round and round. She would then make the brim of the hat, sew it to the crown and buy little imitation buttercups and daisies to put around the brim. It was very comfortable to wear and very light on the head. For the older ladies, she would use darker colours and toques decorating them with cherries or larger flowers. She was quite clever was Auntie Clara, but she could also be quite ruthless.

We used to visit her quite a lot. One day when we went to see them, both Cecil and Joyce's hands were bandaged up. When we asked what had happened, Auntie Clara said that she and Uncle had gone to the shops. On their return, they had found Harry sitting in a chair with a towel around his shoulders. Joyce had a pair of scissors in her hand and Cecil had a lighted taper and was about to singe Harry's hair like he had seen the barbers do when he had been with his father to get his hair cut. Auntie went berserk.

Of course, they hadn't realised the danger they were putting little Harry in but Auntie made sure that they wouldn't play with fire again. She put their two hands on the bars of the iron grate which holds the glowing coals in and burnt them to teach them a lesson. I don't know how she could have done it but she did. I guess she would be put into prison if it happened today.

CHAPTER TWO

1919–1927

SCHOOL DAYS

Liverpool in 1919 was in dire straits and money was very scarce. My father, who worked on the railway, got very little money but Mum made the best of things. We always had good plain meals. She made her own bread which she sent to the local bakers to be baked in his big ovens, twice a week. Mum always gave Nelly, the little shop girl, a penny on Saturday for delivering her loaves of bread.

I began my schooldays at a small church school in Everton Valley called St Mary's. Mum took me for the first fortnight and although it was about 15 minutes walk from Burleigh Road I had to go after that on my own.

One Monday morning Mum asked me if I would call into the baker's on my way to school and give Nelly her penny, as she had missed seeing her on the Saturday. Saying bye-bye, I clutched the penny in my hand and went off to join up with a little friend who went to the same school. Marie had a ½d to spend, so we went into the first sweet shop we came to. I looked longingly at all the different coloured sweets, chocolates and gobstoppers and then I saw them, "Tiger Nuts", those strange-tasting chewy sweet nuts. The lady behind the counter looked at me.

"Do you want some of those, dear?"

I nodded and handed her the penny. To this day, I don't even remember eating those Tiger Nuts. When I arrived home at lunch-time, Mum asked if I had given the penny to Nelly.

"Yes," I answered quickly and went to play with Lol, my baby sister.

After school at 4 o'clock, I arrived home hoping Mum would let me play out a short while before my tea, but she had other ideas. It seems Nelly had called while I was at school and, of course, had disclosed that she hadn't had her penny. I shall never forget my first real punishment. My bloomers were pulled off and Mum put me across her knee. She smacked me until my poor bottom was stinging. I had to go upstairs, get down on my knees and pray to God to forgive me. I then had to get washed and get into bed with no tea or supper. That, Mum said, was not so much for taking the penny, but for telling a lie. I never, ever told her a lie again in all her lifetime.

I stayed at St Mary's school until I was seven and quite enjoyed being there. It was quite an old-fashioned school and I used to stand for an age looking at the stuffed birds and small animals that were in a glass case. The highlight of my life there was the time I won a sweet little peg-doll with a painted face. We had to pay a penny to guess her name and I said Priscilla. I was so proud and kept it many years. Soon after I left, the school was demolished.

*   *   *

The Elementary School I came to when I was seven was only two roads away from my home, which was very handy. On bitter winter mornings when we had to leave the warm school room to go out into the playground for recess, my poor mum would be waiting with a jug of hot cocoa which she would pass to me through the railings for me to share out as best I could. She did this for many years and I shall never forget her kindness.

When I was nine, I had to go to hospital with scarlet fever. I wasn't allowed to see any of my family. It lasted six weeks and was a very trying time for me. One day, the minister from St Mary's church came to see me. He had on a long white hospital gown and he said Mum wanted to know if there was *any thing* I needed. All I could think of was a bright red hair ribbon. A week later this arrived, along with a big hamper full of toys for all the children in the ward from a cousin of Mum's, who was an Assistant Headmistress of a school somewhere in Wavertree.

I had been in hospital for three weeks now and was out of bed. Christmas was in four days. I helped to dress up the Christmas tree with the nurses and to arrange all the toys. Of course, we didn't know what we were getting. The doctor came on Christmas morning and gave us each a present. I got a doll.

The time came to go home. Was it only six weeks? To me it seemed a lifetime. Of course, everything that I had been given had to be left behind because of infection. I didn't mind one bit. I was free. I was going home.

I would like to pass over an episode in my young life which affected me deeply, but as this is a true account of what occurred during my life so I feel that I must not leave it out. I was twelve years old. One of the girls in my class at school took meningitis and died. We had been very good friends and of course, we were all very upset. We brought our own contributions in and teacher bought some lovely flowers. Another girl and I were chosen to take them to Milly's house. Her sorrowing mother opened the door.

"Thank you," she said very quietly, pausing before she added, "would you like to see Milly?"

I hesitated. I had never come face to face with death before, yet I felt it would be churlish to refuse. I nodded my head. How scared I was! We were ushered into the room where poor Milly lay. I stood at the end of the coffin and looked. Her eyes were wide open and her mouth was wide open. It was awful. What lay there bore no resemblance to my poor friend. Over seventy years has now gone by and I remember it as if it were yesterday.

* * *

One day, I came home from school holding my neck.

"What's the matter?" said Mum.

"I've a pain in my neck." She looked and found that I had quite a large lump.

"I think that I'd better take you off to the doctor's," she said.

So off we went. Doctor looked at it and prodded it and I don't think he knew what it was. He told Mum to put a hot poultice on it and if it didn't show any improvement to take me back and he would lance it. We went back home and Mum went into the back-kitchen to make the poultice. She was quite a long time. Eventually, she came into the living room with a long stocking in her hand. In the middle of the stocking she had put a large boiling hot potato. She told me to stand still while she tied it round my neck. I nearly went frantic. The heat was unbelievable. I screamed and screamed and I tried to beat her off with my hands, but she held on making the stocking tighter around my neck. In the end, I just lay sobbing on the settee. Dad came in from work.

"What's the matter?" he asked. Mum told him.

"I'll take it off as soon as it's gone cold," she said. Half an hour later, she took it off. My poor neck was all burned, covered with big red, angry blisters. Mum was too frightened to take me back to the doctor's. She knew that she had done something wrong. Eventually, the blisters got better.

"Well, the lump has gone," Mum triumphantly announced, but to this day I've still got the scars on my neck from that ordeal.

School holidays were great fun. Mum used to make some sandwiches, give us a bottle of milk, a penny for the tram fare and off we would go for the day. We nearly always went with our cousins, Emmie and Kenneth, who lived at 1 Burleigh Road. They were the same ages as Lol and I and the four of us were nearly always together.

In those days, you could go anywhere in Liverpool on the tramcar for a penny return ticket. We used to go to the terminus in prescot and then we would walk for miles and miles through the country lanes. After our picnic, we would pick bluebells etc. We always had a big bunch to bring home. By the time that we arrived back, I guess that we had been out for about eight hours. All for a one penny return! Sometimes we decided to go to the shore at Seaforth but I never enjoyed it as much as Prescot.

With my father working at the railway he could apply for a free pass for a holiday. We always went to the same small boarding house in Blackpool. Miss Hull, the owner, always welcomed us. Mum would buy all our food and Miss Hull would cook it. The bill was itemised as "Room and Attendance". This evidently suited both of them. Every day we went to the shore, paddled and made sand pies. Dad always bought us coloured paper flags to stick in them. We watched

Punch and Judy and every day we got one ice-cream. We were very content and made our own fun. We loved Blackpool. December was quite a busy month for our little family. Mum got Lol and I to clean and stone the dried fruit ready for her to make the bun-loaf and Christmas puddings. You couldn't buy stoneless raisins etc in those days and had to do it yourself. What a sticky job it was! Father used to bring a packet of coloured tissue paper and a pot of glue home and we would sit for hours making paper chains to decorate the walls for Christmas. He was always given a small crate of apples from some kind friend and we would sit and polish those apples until they shone.

About a week before Christmas, we went to the drapers shop to get our presents for Mum and Dad. We must have had about ten shillings in the club now. We usually settled for a tie and handkerchief for Dad and a nice cushion cover or chair-back cover for Mum. We then had to hide them until Christmas Day.

* * *

I must have been about seven when it was discovered that I needed glasses. They were provided free by the education authority and had steel rims. I didn't mind much then. Everybody said they suited me but as I reached my teens, they did give me something of an inferiority complex.

Lol was a lovely sweet natured little girl. She had very thick dark brown, straight hair, cut short with a fringe. She was always very thin. I was more plump, with lighter brown, curly hair, which I wore long. Mum used to worry over Lol because she always had such a white face. One day we went along to the doctor's and Lol was given a thorough examination. Doctor Baxter then turned to Mother.

"There's nothing wrong with her," he said. Then he looked at me and added, "she's the one that you want to watch!" How those words proved to be true.

Around the ages of thirteen and fourteen, I think that I was quite difficult to bring up. I wouldn't eat and I hated dinners, especially Liverpool "Scouse", which we always had on a Monday. We came home from school at lunchtime and Mum put this big dollop of Scouse before me.

"I can't eat it, Mum. I'm not hungry."

"You'll not go back to school until you've eaten it," she said and she meant it. She then went back in the kitchen to do more washing. I just sat there. Poor Lol ate hers and then sat looking at the clock.

"We're going to be late, Marg."

"I don't care," I replied, "I can't eat it."

Lol looked at the kitchen door, grabbed my plate and then gobbled it down. She really was a little love. Just as she returned my plate, Mum came in.

"Now," she said, "you can eat when you try."

Lol often helped me out of scrapes like that. This might have had some effect on my future health for I got almost every disease going and Lol had a fairly healthy life.

*　　*　　*

During our schooldays, Mum's sister, Auntie Emmie, would invite Lol and I to go and stay for a week at her home. She lived in Merton Road, Bootle in a beautiful old house that had gardens back and front, a tennis court, lovely flowers, fruit trees and a small arbor at the bottom of the garden where we could sit. I loved going there but best of all was the bathroom as we only had a tin bath at home as though we loved getting bathed in front of the fire. On the wall of Auntie's bathroom was a framed poem. I would lie in the water and gaze at it, it impressed me so much. I must have been about twelve when I decided to learn it off by heart. This I did and it has played a big part in my life and my children's lives. My son Colin says that it has been his guide through life. This is the poem.

If

If you think you are beaten – you are.
If you think you dare not – you don't.
If you'd like to win, but you think you can't,
It's almost a cinch – you won't.

If you think you are outclassed – you are.
You've got to think high to rise.
You've got to be sure of yourself
before you can even win a prize.

Life's trophies don't always go
to the strongest of fastest man.
The one who wins in the end
is the fellow who thinks he can.

CHAPTER THREE

1927–1939

EARLY WORKING YEARS

From the ages of twelve to fourteen my schooldays were fairly commonplace. I was never exceptionally clever at anything except English and sewing but my school days were happy. I was, though, quite excited about going out to work and finding a job. My first job was at a chandler's shop. I had to mind their baby and scrub the shop's wooden floor. My poor hands were red raw with doing this. The baby was lovely, but he was so big and heavy to carry. I worked really hard there, but I didn't stay long. Looking again for work, I went to the unemployment office in St Thomas Street.

"What do you want to do?" I was asked.

"I would like to be a maid in a big house," I replied. The clerk looked at me.

"Well, a lady wants help. It's a big house near Stanley Park. Take this card with you."

The address was on the card and it was quite near to Liverpool's football ground, at the back end. I knocked at the door and a lady opened it.

"I've come after the job," I said, handing her the card. She asked me into the sitting room.

"You're not very big," she said, "do you think that you could manage these big windows?"

"Oh yes," I said, full of confidence, "I can use a ladder."

"Well," she said, "you can come on a month's trial and see how you go on." I was elated. I ran nearly all the way home.

"I've got a job!" I shouted. Dad was in having his dinner.

"Doing what?" he said quietly.

"I'm going to be a maid in a big house!"

"Oh no you're not. No child of mine is going to be a maid. It's all right for anyone who has no home, but you have a good home. You can go and tell the lady that you can't work for her." I dolefully went and told her and then went back to the unemployment office.

"Would you like to work in a pet shop as a young assistant?"

"Oh yes, I like animals." I felt really happy again. That was until I reached the shop. There on the window in big letters was "Maggots Sold Here." I didn't even go in. Back I went to the unemployment office.

"I'm sorry but I can't work with maggots." Oh dear. She was very patient with me and looked down her list.

"I have a job here which might suit you. It's for a message girl in a very exclusive gown shop in Bold Street. Would you like to apply for that?"

"Oh yes! Thank you, I would like that."

Employment was very hard to come by in those days and I thought that I was very lucky to get a job as a message-girl at such a shop. I was to start on five shillings a week and my task was to dust the big showroom, then go and make a morning cup of tea for the fourteen girls in the workroom who did all the sewing and cutting of the lovely gowns. I was then dispatched with various pieces of coloured material clutched in my hand and had to buy reels of silk to match them perfectly. I had to go from shop to shop doing this for if it was a bad match I was sent back. At five o'clock, I was told to go down to the showroom to take the mail.

On my first day, I went in by the front entrance and was very politely told that everybody entered that way and left the shop at six o'clock that way, but that I was to use the back entrance only for all my messages. This I did. The back entrance was down five wooden steps into Back Newington and as I entered the showroom a lovely girl was standing before a long mirror combing her hair.

"Hello," she said, "are you the new girl?"

"Yes," I answered shyly.

"Well, I'm Betty," she said. "I do the modelling. If you go up those stairs, you will find Phyllis who will be doing the parcels for the post."

It was a long showroom. The theme was blue and gold. Fresh flowers were arranged in various designs and not a gown nor a coat was to be seen. The walls seemed to have mirrors all round but behind those mirrors were the long white wardrobes which contained the garments.

I went up the staircase with its soft blue carpet to the top showroom. Miss Robina Robinson, the owner of the shop, had her office on this floor. She was a small, very petite and also very astute business woman. She went to Paris twice a year to buy gowns and to attend the shows of the very best known Parisian designers. Phyllis had the post ready for me, four gown boxes. I went downstairs into the back part of the shop, opened the door and stepped out – into nothing. The steps had gone. I lay on the ground having fallen to my knees. My new stockings were torn, my knees were bleeding. It was pouring with rain and the parcels lay scattered around me.

"Are you all right, luv?" A voice sounded in my ear and then I felt myself being lifted up. It was a very kind workman from Van Greissan's, the piano shop next door. "What did you do? Didn't you know the cleaner takes the steps in as soon as she comes?" he said.

"No, I didn't know." I picked up the parcels. They were wet and a bit dirty but it was only the brown paper. I guessed the boxes would be all right underneath and off I went to the post office in Mount Pleasant. So ended my first day at work.

After the first few days, things became a whole lot easier. I knew my way around town, got on well in the workroom and knew everybody by name. The one job that I wasn't keen on doing was picking up the pins, but being the youngest one there I had this to do. I was given a magnet and a box and I had to go down on all fours and pick up every pin in the two workrooms.

Miss Jarrett, the head girl over the workrooms, was a thin, erratic nervous type. She was very bad-tempered and easily upset. Everybody seemed to be frightened of her but she certainly knew her job.

Mornings were my busiest time. After I had done all the messages for the staff, my time was my own until almost five o'clock when I went for the post. One afternoon at about half-past one I went into the showroom.

"Could I see Miss Robinson, please?" I asked Miss Osborne, the manageress. She looked at me askance.

"Very well. She's in her office." I went up to the top showroom, across the floor and knocked at the door.

"Come in," a voice spoke. I went in and Miss Robinson looked quite kindly at me.

"Well, Margery, what can I do for you?" I looked at her steadily.

"Could I have the afternoon off, please?" I said. She bent her head.

"How long have you been here?" she asked.

"Two weeks."

"And what do you want the time off for?"

"I want to go to the cinema to see 'Nurse Edith Cavell'," I said very carefully. It never occurred to me to lie. Mother always drilled into me to tell the truth. She looked astonished, yet a little bit amused. "I've been saving up my pocket money so I could go one day," I told her.

"Well," she smiled, "I'll let you go for your cheek, but be back for five to take the post." From that day on, Miss Robinson always was very nice to me.

*   *   *

Miss Robinson had two pets. One was a black and white French Bulldog called Bill and the other was a Siamese cat called Chang. They were both very spoilt. Bill was fed on best English raw beef and Chang had a collar and lead and would go out with Miss Robinson to lunch walking very proudly by her side just like a dog. One day, I was called into the office. Miss Robinson was sitting there.

"Margery," she said, "have you had your lunch?"

"Yes," I replied.

"Well, it's a lovely day. Would you like to take Bill to West Kirby for the afternoon and give him a run on the sands?"

"Oh, yes!" I said.

"Well, be back at five-thirty to take the post."

I was delighted. We had a lovely day and this was only the

start of it. We had many happy days at West Kirby. There was no underground Mersey Railway in those days. The trains which left Central Station had a corridor with small compartments which sat about ten people when full, five seats facing each other on each side. The upholstery was in velvet and it was very comfortable. In the afternoon the train was fairly empty and we nearly always managed to get an empty compartment to ourselves. Bill would jump on the seat and when I sat down he would sit on my knee. He was a big, heavy lump, but I didn't mind. He always looked so happy and knew where he was going. The railway guards at Central knew me quite well and they always gave me a big smile.

The only flaw to this arrangement was when I went on messages to the shop. I always had Bill with me and when we went down Bold Street and came to the part which led into the station, Bill would sit down and wouldn't budge. I would pull the lead and try to drag him, but he wouldn't move. He wanted to go to West Kirby. In the end, I had to carry him until we were well past.

I'll never forget one afternoon. We were joyfully on our way to the train when Bill suddenly sat down in the middle of the station to do his business. I felt mortified. I was so ashamed I had to stand there holding his lead with my head down. When I then saw a pair of legs standing by me I looked up and there was one of the railway guards, hands on his hips, looking down at Bill and me.

"I'm . . . I'm so sorry," I stammered. I wished the earth would swallow me up. When Bill finished I looked at the pile and then looked at the guard. His mouth twitched.

"Go get your train, girlie," he said, "I'll see to this mess." I thought what a nice kind man he was.

I had been ten months at the gown shop when I was told to

go up to the office. Miss Robinson asked me if I would like to learn to be a dressmaker. She said Miss Jarret had said she would like me in the workroom. Of course I was delighted and said so, but she said that I would have to talk it over with my mother. My wages would still only be five shillings a week for two years, go up to seven shillings a week and then increase each year until I was a fully fledged dressmaker, which would take seven years. Mum was quite pleased. She had heard that some gown shops even charged a premium of five shillings a week for such training.

I really enjoyed my life in the workroom. I learned how to do buttonholes, hems, binding and tucking. I was a very apt pupil and Miss Jarrett seemed pleased with me. I got a week's holiday in my first year. I was there over two years learning dressmaking. There were two work rooms, each containing eight girls and we sat at a long table. Miss Jarrett did all the cutting out of the gowns and the girls did the rest. We used to make ball gowns for the debutantes when they were presented to the *Queen* Mary, wife of King George. I used to help embroider some of the long trains. All of the pearls and tiny crystal beads were sewn on by hand.

I used to make Miss Robinson's chiffon nightdresses. Each one had sixty pin tucks all done by hand. Imagine drawing a thread in chiffon eighteen inches long and then every ½ inch between another thread and hand sewing sixty tucks. It used to take a long time, but the result was good. There were now two other apprentices in the workroom and also the message girl.

One day, I was asked to go to Miss Robinson's office and went in trepidation, wondering what I had done.

"Sit down, Margery," she said. "Now, how would you like to come into the showroom and learn to be an assistant?" I was dumbfounded. I couldn't believe it. She said that Miss Osborne who was the manageress of the showroom would like me to. I knew it was a big lift in position and prestige but I had made such a lot of friends in the workrooms.

"Talk it over with your mother and let me know," she said.

I started in the Showroom the following Monday and Miss Jarrett was furious. When she came down to do a fitting, she wouldn't look at me. Miss Osborne said my job was to see the ladies into the fitting rooms and to help Betty, who was in charge of the mannequins on which the dresses were shown. It was very interesting and I knew I was going to like it. When my lunch hour came, I went up to the workroom to have my lunch with the girls. Of course, there was a bit of chaff.

"Oh, we thought you'd be too stuck up now to come and eat with us." I laughed.

"Don't be daft," I said as they made room for me at the table.

Later that day, I was busy hanging up a few gowns when one of the apprentices came into the showroom and said that Miss Jarrett wanted me in the workroom. It was now five thirty. Miss Osborne looked askance at her, but said I could go. Miss Jarrett stood at the top of the stairs, the pin box and a magnet in her hand.

"Pick up the pins," she said, handing me the box. I looked at her. Everybody went very quiet. The two apprentices were doing nothing. I went down on my knees on the bare wooden floor and started to pick up the pins. The tears were rolling down my face, but I kept my head down so that she wouldn't see. The dressmakers, my friends, were very supportive.

"Never mind, kid."

"Isn't she a pig!"

"Never mind, love." Each one whispered something to me. I did both workrooms and then took the box over to her.

"Anything else, Miss Jarrett?" I asked. She uttered a gruff "No," but she looked very shame-faced.

Miss Osborne was outraged when she asked what I was wanted for, but I told her not to make an issue of it. It was best forgotten. Miss Jarrett was just mad at losing one of her girls.

*   *   *

I was seventeen when I became aware that a boy was following me around. He used to stand at the top of Burleigh Road just in the hope of seeing me. I mentioned it to my mother and being very wise she told me that she would like to meet him. Both my mum and dad liked Alf Beswick, so when he took me to see his mum and dad it was taken for granted that we were courting.

Alf had one sister, Bella, and three brothers, Charlie, Billy, who married a nice girl called Marie, and Peter, who married Nancy. I became very fond of them all. They were a lovely family and always gave me a welcome.

With having a knowledge of sewing, I could do some alterations for people, such as hems, shortening sleeves etc. One day a young lady came and asked if I could make her a dress.

"Of course," I said. I was always very sure of myself. It had a full flare skirt, a plain bodice and short sleeves and was too be called for at about five o'clock in ten days time. When it was finished I was quite pleased with it. I put the iron on to press it and started on the bodice first, having slipped the dress over the ironing board. I put the iron on the front of the bodice and couldn't believe it. A big hole in the shape of the iron appeared as the material just dissolved with the heat. Poor Mum looked horrified.

"Oh Margery! What will you do?" she asked.

I was so stunned I didn't answer. I looked at the clock. I had half an hour. I quickly sorted out the pieces of material and found what I wanted – a triangular piece. I cut out the burnt part and inserted the other piece and Lo! the first cowl neck was born. The lady was very pleased. If only she had known what had really happened.

At this stage in my life I was always well dressed. Miss Robinson gave me all her clothes when she had finished with them as I was small like her. I had a few pure silk dresses and one lovely suit. They had all been bought in Paris. She really was a very kind lady and I was very lucky to be working there at all. In those days Bold Street was like Bond Street in London. Next door to our shop was Fuller's, a high class restaurant. The meals there were very expensive. Opposite our shop was "Bacon's." They sold wonderful gowns, marvelous hats and beautiful fur coats of chinchilla, sable, fox and ermine. They had two large workrooms just making hats alone. It was big business in those days. My cousin, Doris, who was eight years older than me, worked there. She was a milliner and we were very good friends. Doris and I walked to work together everyday. We took a short cut through Great Homer Street Market, came through a small lane and came out by the Walker Art Gallery. After that, it was only a short way to Bold Street. We always returned home by tram-car.

1932 was a very traumatic year. One day Miss Robinson called all of the workroom staff and all of the showroom staff together. She told us that she was giving up the business and going to live in London. She said she was very sorry to do this, but we were all on a month's notice. For me, this was dreadful news.

My dear father then became very ill. The doctor diagnosed

carcinoma of the lungs and he was only given a short time left to live.

Finally, Doris, my cousin whom I thought so much of, got tuberculosis of the throat. She was very ill and, after a short illness, died when she was twenty-seven. I was broken-hearted.

We were not going to tell Dad, with him being so very ill, but when Mum went up with some soup for him, he said, "Doris has gone!" A fortnight later, my Aunt Agnes, another of my mother's sisters, called and we were having some lunch. Suddenly, we heard a knock on the ceiling. We had given Dad a walking stick to knock on the floor if he wanted anything. I ran upstairs. Poor Dad said something. I couldn't make out what it was. Then his head fell back and I shouted.

"Mum!" She came running up the stairs, my aunt behind her. She put her arms around him.

"Oh! Edgar," she said. My aunt roughly pulled her from Dad.

"Let him go. Don't bring him back," she cried. My poor dear Mum, with tears streaming down her cheeks, knelt by the bed and with her voice faltering on every word, recited the Lord's Prayer all the way through. I thought that she was so brave to do that.

I was devastated. My father had just died aged fifty-two, Doris had died and I had no job. Lol had just started work at 5/-a week and Mum only got 10/-a week widow's pension. The rent alone was 12/6 a week and I knew I had to do something. After five years at Robina Robinson's my wages had been 14/- shillings a week. I went to the unemployment agency and explained my position. I just had to get a job paying at least 30/- shillings.

I'd had some very happy times at Robina Robinson's and I was very sorry to leave. I managed to get a job as manageress of a small gown shop in Derby Lane called Doreen's at 32/6 a week. This was a big help to Mum, but it was still very difficult to manage moneywise.

The shop had originally been a house and had a small frontage with the fitting rooms up the stairs. I was there nearly four years. There were three of us on the staff, myself, Gaynor Dodd, my assistant, and Pat Kelly. Miss Nelson, who owned the shop, did all the buying. I would dress the window and do all the fittings. Both Gaynor and I would do the selling of the garments and Pat did all the alterations to the coats and dresses. Our hours were from nine until six and we all worked very hard and never refused a sale. If a customer wanted her dress shortening we did it at once no matter how late the time. At Easter and Christmas time it was not unknown for us all to stay up until nearly two o'clock in the morning finishing off the alterations. Miss Nelson would then take us home in her car. Our Christmas gift from Miss Nelson was always a dress of our own choosing, but we certainly deserved it.

One Wednesday morning, Miss Nelson phoned me to ask if I would shut up shop and take the cash home as she was taking her little niece Pamela to Blackpool for the day. Next morning she rang to say that she wouldn't be in for a few days. Her shattering news was that little Pamela was dead! It seems that when they arrived at her sister Ruby's home, her sister had called to Pamela but got no answer. She was just sitting in a corner and wouldn't speak. They put her in the car and took her to the doctor's. He immediately rang the hospital, but sadly, she died at nine o'clock. She had loba-pneumonia, a virus which turns everything to water. Even after death, Miss Nelson said her head had swollen to twice its size and had to be lanced to let the water out.

Gaynor, Pat and I became very good friends. I had been going out with Alf now for about four years and when his twenty-first birthday came around his mum decided to give him a big party. We were all there and it was at the party that Gaynor met Alf's eldest brother, Charlie. They eventually married and went to live in Scotland. They had two lovely little girls, Ann and Jan. So my best friend was to become my sister-in-law. Gaynor's brother, Stan, met Bella, Alf's sister. They got married and had two children, Margaret and Graham. So, sister and brother married sister and brother. So I guess that I've a lot to answer for. It's good to know that they were all so happy.

Alf was a regular visitor now to our house. He came one day looking very smart in a new trilby hat. When he came in he carefully put it on top of the parrot's cage. When it came time for him to go he looked in dismay at his hat. The parrot had bitten seven holes in the brim. I couldn't help laughing, but I felt so sorry for him.

We had that bird quite a few years and I could have loved him but he really hated me. He would scream if I went near the cage. He liked Mum and Lol and he loved Dad. Sometimes he sat on Dad's shoulder, but if I came in from school and he was out of the cage, he would chase and bite meand I would run up the stairs screaming. He used to try and get up the stairs, but Dad would grab him and put him back in his cage. Perhaps he knew that Alf was my boyfriend and that was why he destroyed his hat.

Alf and I joined a hiking club and went out most weekends. It was formed by Old Scholars of Venice Street School. There

I met up again with one of my friends, Flo Titherington and we had some good outings. Flo has done some writing herself and is a member of the Liverpool Literary Club. She goes each year for a week's holiday to Swanick and meets all the top writers of this era. I dread to think what she will say about my modest offering. Lol was now working at Bunney's, a large shop on the corner of Whitechapel. Lol was in the stationery department and seemed to be quite happy there making many friends.

Liverpool had many wonderful shops: Hendersons, Bon Marche etc. Opposite Bunney's was Cooper's. It was a shop that specialised in exotic foreign foods, which were very expensive, there was always a lovely smell of coffee coming from there. I enjoyed walking through Cooper's. As you went through the door the first thing your eyes would see were the jars and jars of different types of coffee. The tea counter was the same. At the delicatessen counter I couldn't move. I would look at all the different mousses, tiny fishes and all kinds of pickled things and their smell was out of this world. I couldn't buy anything, but it cost nothing to look.

*   *   *

One Sunday in 1933 after church, the curate said to Mum that if she found a house with a bathroom, he would move in as a lodger. So after nineteen years in the same house, we moved into the next road, Burleigh Road South. It was a much larger house with five bedrooms, a bathroom and a cellar. I was never happy about it but Mr Cragg the curate, came to live with us. I didn't like him very much either. I was still keeping company with Alf and when I would see him to the door it had to be a quick kiss as Mum would be shouting for me to come in. Yet she would often go to bed and leave me up with Mr Cragg, who now and again would try to put his arm around me. I wasn't having any and kept my distance.

One morning Mr Cragg approached my mother.

"When I was kneeling down saying prayers last night," he said, "I felt something on my neck. It was a bug."

"Oh no!" Mum replied.

"Yes, I think this house has got bugs in it."

That night Lol and I and the curate went up to the two attic bedrooms on the top floor and, yes, there were bugs on the walls, little round smelly things. It was awful and our other house had been so clean. Mum told the landlord and he had the whole house fumigated, but it was no good. The bugs came back, Mr Cragg left and we moved into a nice house in another part of Anfield.

I went to work one morning in 1934 feeling quite ill and Miss Nelson took me home. I was in hospital by that evening with diphtheria. I was twenty-one but was put in a ward full of children. It is a loathsome disease and it was very rife at the time. My home and the shop where I worked had to be stove-fumigated. I was in hospital for six weeks. After three weeks in bed, I was allowed to get up and walk around the grounds. I was only allowed to see Alf once in the grounds and he had to put on protective gear. I don't know what he thought of me, all they could provide for me to wear was a sun-bonnet and a little gym-slip. I was the only adult there. The hospital only had children's clothes and of course you had to wear what they provided because of the infection. I was glad when I was able to return home.

1936 was the year that Alf and I were going to be married, but Alf's mum asked if we would wait until the next year. She had bought a bedroom suite on the weekly and said she needed

Alf's weekly contribution. We agreed, but decided to go on holiday together to Warren Point in Ireland.

I remember it was a very rough crossing and the boat was pitching and tossing when we went down below for lunch. I noticed an old man who looked really ill and mentioned it to Alf. He didn't answer and I looked at him. His face was green.

"Sorry," he said and rushed out of the dining room. I didn't see him again until we reached Ireland.

It does indeed live up to its name, "The Emerald Isle"; everywhere is a beautiful shade of green. We stayed at a large farm. There were tennis courts, lovely gardens and if you wanted to have your meals in the gardens, it was no problem. It was a very free and easy place. It was run by two brothers and you could come in when you liked. When you did come in there was a huge iron pan on an open fire, filled with boiled potatoes in their jackets, a big pot of butter and glasses of milk and you just helped yourself. It was the same with the sleeping arrangements, nobody minded who slept with who. So, Alf and I slept together. We decided not to abuse our parents trust in us and so we just put our arms around each other and went to sleep. It was no great hassle really. We played tennis, walked long walks down the lovely country lanes and danced in the gardens at night. We were always tired out when we went to bed.

Some days we went out in a jolting cart. This was a small cart driven by one horse and I really enjoyed that. We also went to Newry market on market day. It makes me feel sad when I hear about all the bombing and riots that have gone on in that lovely country.

*   *   *

5th June, 1937 was the day that Alf and I got married and it began to rain just as we came out of the church. The reception was held at Mrs Beswick's house and we had a lovely time.

"Come on Betty, get on that piano," someone shouted. Betty Barnes, who was a friend of Bella's, was a very stout lady, but could she play that piano? She was marvellous. My cousin Les, who gave me away, went down into the cellar with Bill Beswick to put some big beams to bolster the ceiling in case the floor gave way. Pop Beswick, Alf's dad, was a very quiet man. I liked him a lot. He would just sit smiling at everybody and have his pint. Mum and Alf's mum got on very well together. Mum was a very good cook and Mrs Beswick, too, always kept a "good table".

Alf and I went to Blankenburg in Belgium for our honeymoon. It was very new and exciting to go abroad in those days. We enjoyed it very much, but I didn't like the food. To me the vegetables were always too sweet, as was the chocolate.

We went walking through the town of Blankenburg looking at the shops and then gasped. The next shop window was full of coffins!

We spent a day at the beautiful old city of Bruges. We decided to go inside "The Church of the Holy Blood". As I hadn't a hat with me, Alf pulled his handkerchief out of his pocket to put on my head. I guess you know what happened, his pocket was full of confetti. Were our faces red!

Alf and I lived with mum and Lol for a short time, but soon felt it was time to move to a place of our own. We found a nice house in Gordon Drive in Knotty Ash with a garden back and front for 18/-a week. I was pregnant. Mum managed to get a smaller house with less rent and, with Lol working at Bunny's, they could just manage. Shortly before Colin was born, I had salmonella and had to go into hospital. Salmonella is a poison that goes right through the blood stream. However, I got over it and the baby was all right. Times were very difficult. Alf only got £3 a week and I was paying nine shillings a week to Derwent House for our furniture. Alf was a dental mechanic and worked with a dentist in Allerton. His expenses for fares etc, came to 7/6 a week. That left me exactly £1/5/6 for everything: food, Lux for the nappies, soap, baby powder, coal, gas and electricity. I often wonder how I managed. I took in sewing and stayed up very late, night after night, doing alterations. It did help the money situation a bit, though.

Mum used to come and see me on a Tuesday and nearly always gave me two shillings. She was so kind. I often had no money when she came. With the money she gave to me, I would buy some bones from the butcher and few vegetables and make a big pan of soup which would do us for a few days.

I looked forward to Saturday nights. Nana and Pop Beswick used to come to see their first grandchild. So did Billy and Bella and they always brought the supper for us all – roast bacon ribs. Were they lovely? I don't think I ever enjoyed anything as much as those ribs.

*　　*　　*

About six months after I got married, I started to get a pain in my big right toe. Alf and I quite liked dancing, but I found that it became worse after a dance session. I would be sitting comfortably at home when suddenly I would jump up.

"Ouch! Oh, my toe!" Alf advised me to see a chiropodist, so off I went. He looked at my toe and felt it. It was quite stiff.

"Nothing I can do, dear," he said, "I think that you had better see a doctor." Off I went to the doctor. He looked at it and felt it. It was rigid.

"There's nothing I can do. I'll give you a note for the hospital," he said. Off I went to the Northern Hospital. I saw a specialist.

"Oh, you'll have to come in for a couple of days," I was told. I still didn't know what was wrong with my big toe. A week later I got a letter to go in and it was quite nice really. I didn't feel ill and the nurses were fun. Next morning nurse came with a bowl of warm water and a small scrubbing brush.

"I'm going to scrub your feet now," she said. I was indignant.

"They're not dirty!"

"I know dear, but you're having your operation this afternoon and I have to get you ready." Well, have you ever had your feet scrubbed? I was hysterical. I laughed and laughed.

"Stop it!" I said. She was laughing too. When she had finished, she put long white stockings on both my legs. I went down to the operating theater and felt what I thought were drops of water falling on my face. Then I blacked out. When I came to I was very sick and for the next twelve hours I felt quite ill. It seems that ether, the anesthetic used in those days, had that effect on everybody. I had a cage over my legs and after five days it was removed and the sister came to take the stitches out. She took the bandages off and I looked at my poor toe. It was at right-angles to the rest of my foot. "Goodness," I thought, "I'll never get a shoe on!" The surgeon came into the ward.

"How are you?" he said.

"I'm all right, thank you." He gently touched my toe.

"Does it hurt?"

"No," I said quite brightly. He then got hold of it and gave it a big twist. I nearly hit the ceiling.

"I bet that did," he said with a smile. I could have hit him.

I looked down at my foot and what was a big toe was now a little toe.

"What was the matter with it?" I asked.

"Well,' he said, "the large bone was diseased, so I had to remove it."

I was in hospital for ten days and it was very painful putting my foot down for a very long time afterwards.

CHAPTER FOUR

1939–1945

THE WAR YEARS

In August 1939 Alf came home from work with the news that his boss, Mr P, had asked him if he would be willing for the three of us to go and live with him and his wife in Heswall for a short while. The authorities were inquiring in Heswall as to who would be eligible to take in evacuees and as the Ps had no children and a large house, their name would definitely be on the list should war have broken out. If we were there they would not be considered. I definitely didn't want to go and didn't want to leave my nice little home. However, I thought that it would leave Alf in a bit of a difficult position, so I decided to go. We went, that Thursday night, October 31st, in Mr P's car, with a large suitcase packed with out clothes and gas masks. The baby's gas bask was a very large affair and he had to go right inside it.

When we arrived I was introduced to Mrs P and I knew right away we wouldn't get on. She was bossy and looked down her nose at me despite the fact Alf and I were doing her a favour. She said she thought we would feel better if we lived in the kitchen but we would all eat together in the dining room. She would do all the cooking and I could do the washing-up but added she was very particular about her pans.

"So am I," I said, "you can see your face in my pans!" I went into the kitchen and looked in dismay at the two easy chairs. They both had a big hole in the seat. I didn't sit on the edge of the chair I would fall through the hole. "Alf. We've left our lovely little home for this," I said. He tried to comfort me.

"It won't be for long, Margert." Next morning, Friday 1st November 1939, Mrs P came into the kitchen.

"When you've fed the baby, you can take him out until 1 o'clock. Then you can feed him, have your lunch and go out again until 5 o'clock when you can bath and feed the baby and get him to bed before the men come in."

It was quite evident that she did not want my baby around. Colin was twenty-one pounds at nine months old, so you can guess how very tired I was having to carry him around all day that day. On Saturday, Mr P brought Colin's high pram over with some clean blankets and lots of other items. I looked at Alf.

"It looks as if we are here for months," I said.

"It may not be for long," he said.

Sunday morning, September 3rd, I got up early, dressed Colin and wrote a note to Mrs P saying that I was unhappy and was going home. I pushed the note under her bedroom door. I looked in on Alf who was still asleep. I crept out of the house and off I went. It was a lovely morning. It had been raining earlier, but now the sun was shining and the sky looked so blue. I pushed Colin along in his pram and felt so pleased with myself. I was almost at Heswall railway station when I heard a shout. I looked around and there was Alf, tearing along, a coat over his pyjamas.

"Marg, come back!" I had to stop. He begged me to go back

and I felt so sorry for him, for it did put him in a difficult situation.

"What was the matter?" Mrs P asked when we returned to the house.

"I wasn't happy," I said.

"Well," she replied, "you've got a bloody sight more to be unhappy about now! War has been declared!"

I stayed until the following Thursday when Mrs P was going to Liverpool and I made my escape. I found out the times of the buses, dressed Colin and off we went. I went to Alf's mum's house first. Then Bella came back to Gordon Drive with me. She rang Alf to tell him I was home. Nobody blamed me for doing what I did. About six months later the Ps left Heswall.

* * *

Alf got work in Napier's making war components and as it was war work, he was exempt from going into the forces. My sister Lol got married to Charlie Winrow who was a private in the army. They were married in Nottingham. I couldn't go for I was heavily pregnant with David. One day later, Charlie was posted abroad and Lol didn't see him for four years.

She went to work at Napiers also. Everybody was expected to do their utmost to help the war effort. Women were drafted to do all the jobs men used to do. They went on the buses, worked in the Land Army, went on the munitions, fire watching etc. Only mothers looking after children were exempt.

May 1941 was a month I will never forget. How Liverpool suffered! Night after night the incessant bombing. Mill Road Maternity Hospital was hit. A shelter full of people got a direct hit. There were many deaths. Our house in Gordon Drive was on the fringe of the city. We didn't get it quite so bad but one night the front door was blown off and our windows were shattered. The lights went out and Colin and I were covered with soot. This was due to the blast from a bomb that had dropped in a road nearby. Alf was out on his Home Guard duties.

My second son, David, was born on the 31st May. I was in an Anderson Shelter, a small family shelter dug deep in the garden when my pains started. There were about five small steps to go down. Alf had made a very narrow bench for us to sit on. That night, Mum came to keep me company. Colin was now two-and-a-half years old. The three of us had been in the shelter for about an hour.

"I can't stand this, Mum. I'm getting out," I said. I had another spasm of pain. The three of us had just got into the living room when Alf arrived on his motor-bike.

"Why aren't you in the shelter?"

"I think that you had better go for the midwife, Alf," said Mum. Alf went and returned very quickly with the midwife.

"Well dear," she said, "we'll go upstairs and I'll have a look at you. I don't suppose that it'll happen for a couple of hours yet." I got on the bed. Mum poked her head around the bedroom door.

"If you want me for anything, Nurse, just let me know."

"I do," said the nurse, "Hold her leg. The baby's coming now." I couldn't believe it. I had another little son and so quickly. The midwife said that she had never delivered such a clean baby.

"He hardly wants washing," was her comment.

"I guess it's because I took liquid Paraffin every day for the best part of three months," I said with a grin. We called him David. He was a lovely baby and very good, just like Colin.

When Dave was four months old, Mother and my sister, Lol,

came to visit me. Lol didn't seem very well and when it was time for them to leave, it was evident that they couldn't go. She seemed quite ill. I put Mum and Lol in the front bedroom. The next day we called the doctor in. Poor Lol was very ill with pneumonia. This lasted three whole weeks. Mum stayed to look after her. Alf and I and the two children slept in the back bedroom.

One morning after Alf had left for work and Colin had gone to school, I told Mum that I didn't feel very well.

"Oh dear," said Mum, "what's the matter?"

"I don't know. My head feels funny."

"Well, you'd better go and get into bed with Lol. I'll look after the baby." In the afternoon, Lol's brother-in-law, Ernie Winrow, came to visit her. He was a nice chap, who was in the Royal Air Force. "You can go upstairs," said Mum, "the two of them are in bed. I don't know what's the matter with Marg." Ernie came in the room with some grapes for Lol.

"Hello," he said, "what's this?" He smiled at us both. Lol was pleased to see him and was now feeling a lot better. He didn't stay long but, when he went downstairs, he told Mum that he thought that she should ring for the doctor to come and see me. When the doctor came, he told Mum I was very ill and must go to hospital immediately. I had loba-pneumonia, the same virus that had killed Miss Nelson's niece Pamela a few years earlier. Just as the ambulance arrived, Alf came up on his motor-bike. Alf and Mum came to Whiston Hospital with me. As soon as I got there, they sent for the minister and he came very quickly. He was very kind and said some prayers and asked God if it was his wish to spare my life.

After Mum and Alf had left, the sister of the ward brought in three large syphons of soda water and told me that I must keep drinking all night.

"I know that you will bring it back," she said, "but you must drink all of this by morning." She then gave me some M & B pills. A nurse stayed with me all night to give me the soda water and I'm sure that with their care they saved my life.

Next morning I was put by the door in a very unusual bed. It was very high and the back of the bed was wound up. I had to sit up all day and night. The ward sister said that I must never lie down. Every bed in the ward had a wire cage underneath. During an air-raid, everybody had to lie down, the cage was then put over them and then the nurses brought bed mattresses in and put one over each cage. This was to protect the patient from any glass which might get shattered. Of course, I was just left because I could not lay down. One night there was a new probationary nurse on duty. The sirens went off. Everybody lay down. This new nurse bustled in. As my bed was near the door she came to me first.

"Come on, lie down," she said as she started to wind the bed down.

"I don't lie down," I said in a very weak voice.

"No," said the lady in the next bed, "she always sits up."

"Nonsense!" said the nurse. "Everybody must lay down."

Of course, there was no cage under my bed. So the nurse went out and brought one of the heavy mattresses in. I felt quite ill lying down but when she put the mattress on top of me with no cage I thought that I was dying. I couldn't breathe. I think that I would have died but for the lady in the next bed. She started to shout for sister and the next few minutes were frantic. My bed was wound up. The doctor came and he gave me something to drink and I felt a bit better. I couldn't really blame the nurse. She was only doing what she had been told to do.

Eventually, I survived this awful illness and was so pleased to get home to my family.

At the age of two Dave was a little rascal. He was a good child but he wanted a lot of watching. He had a habit of putting things in his mouth. One time I left him in Alf's care in the bedroom while I went downstairs to cook a meal. Alf finished what he was doing and came down. After a short while I looked around.

"Where's Dave?" I asked.

"Oh," he said, "I forgot him."

I rushed upstairs. Dave was sitting on the floor with my little trinket box on his knee. He was just about to put something into his mouth. I wasn't taking any chances and took him downstairs giving him a big dose of Castor Oil. I rang the doctor and asked for his advice. He said that I had done the right thing but if he seems to have any pains to contact him immediately. Dave was all right, but he passed five pearl buttons and three pieces of coal which he must have got out of the tiny grate in the room. A few months later he swallowed the leg of an alarm clock which I gave him to listen to. I went through the same procedure as before and very luckily it was passed the same way. I thank God for Castor Oil.

A little Scottish girl called Primrose used to take Dave for walks in his little go-chair. One day she called to take him out, but he was quite poorly. I was so very worried about him. He just wouldn't take the tablets the doctor ordered. I told him that I had tried squashing them up in a drink and also mixing them with a bit of jam but he spat them out every time. Even the doctor tried but it was no use. They were M & B tablets and the doctor said that if he didn't take them, he would have to go into hospital as he was on the verge of pneumonia. Primrose really loved him and was so upset when I told her this. She said to give the tablets to her. She went into the room.

'How's ma wee boy?' she said kissing him, 'have a sweetie

from Prim." He took the tablet off her and ate it. Every three hours he took the "sweetie" from Prim. She stayed all night. Next morning he was ever so much better. After three days he was on the road to recovery. So much must be said for child psychology.

* * *

1943 proved to be a very disturbing and traumatic year for me. I didn't see much of Alf. After he finished work and had had his dinner he was off to the Home Guard on his motorbike. He was the dispatch rider for them in our district. Colin had started school so I had plenty to do taking him back and forth each day, looking after David and taking in as much sewing as I could to make a few extra shillings. When bedtime came around I would drop into bed exhausted. I never heard Alf come in. He was always very late and most times I would be asleep.

There came a period when Alf had to do nights at Napiers' making plane components. We began to see less and less of each other. One night after our meal, he told me that he had fallen in love with Dora, a girl at his works. It is very hard to put into words how I felt. My world seemed to have fallen apart and crushed me. I wanted to die: my two little boys, my home, my love for him, all our years together since we were seventeen. His voice came as if through a mist.

"I'm sorry, Marg. I can't help it. I love her." We carried on just living. I still cooked and looked after his well being but that was all. He was full of remorse but he wouldn't give her up. Poor Mum was shattered. She always loved Alf. His family were also very upset for they all loved me. His dad came and did his best to try and remonstrate with Alf.

"What's Margery done?"

"Marg has done nothing," said Alf, "it's just me. I've fallen in love."

"Well, you've just got to get over it," said his father. "You've a lovely wife, two little boys, a lovely home. What more can you want?" But it was no use. Alf just went on seeing Dora. It was a very sad time.

One day I had a note from Dovecot School to go to see Colin's teacher. When I went in to see her, the nurse was there also.

"Mrs Beswick," she said. "Colin is a lovely little boy, but he is hyper sensitive and we can't nail it down to anything. Is his father in the army?"

"No," I replied.

"Have you any other children?"

"A little boy of two and a half."

"Maybe he is jealous."

"No, he loves him. I don't show any favouritism."

"Well," she said, "there is something troubling him. If I was you, I would give him as much love as you can, even nurse him. Sit him on your knee."

"I will."

I thanked her. I knew what it was, but how could I tell her of the times when, with tears streaming down my face, a little hand would hold mine and a little voice would say "Daddy don't you love Mummy anymore?" to a father who sat with his head in his hands saying "Sorry, I can't help it."

These were terrible times. I couldn't dislike Alf. I felt sorry for him, sorry for my little boys who loved him and sorry for myself also.

Three years passed.

"Marg, will you divorce me?" Alf asked.

"Can you honestly give up your two little boys, Alf?" I replied.

"Yes, I will have to."

"Well, I'm not staying here. If you will see us safely moved to another house nearer to my mother, I will divorce you when you are ready."

We advertised to exchange houses in the Anfield area and didn't have to wait very long. Soon we were installed in a house in Richmond Park, about ten minutes walk from Mum's. Alf came with us until he was ready to leave. I would cook his dinner but he slept in the small bedroom on his own. We were friendly and spoke to each other, but he was out nearly every night. I knew that I would have to get a job when Alf left. The rent was 18 shillings a week. Of course, he would have to keep the boys.

One night after his dinner, he said that he and Dora were going to the Empire to see a musical comedy and Dora had suggested that I could go with them if my Mum would mind the boys.

"You never go out," he said.

"I don't know Alf. I'd have to think it over." Mum was all for it.

"You go, Marg. It will be a change for you." I told Alf that I would go.

The night arrived.

"Dora will meet us in the foyer," Alf said.

After a quick snack, we left together. When we arrived at the Empire, Dora wasn't there. We waited and waited. Eventually Alf said that something must have delayed her. He handed me a ticket.

"You go and get your seat and we'll join you as soon as she arrives."

I went up into the dress circle. It was a lovely seat, right in the centre of the second row. The lights dimmed, the show started. No-one came. The tears rolled down my cheeks. I sat and sat on my own, silently sobbing. I couldn't tell you what the show was about. All I could see was the two empty seats alongside me. At the end of the show I hurried out, head down in case anyone saw my grief-stricken face. I quickly got a bus. I wanted to get home. Mum opened the door.

"Oh, Mum, they didn't come!" I sobbed. I don't think that I have ever seen her so angry. She made me some hot cocoa.

"Now go to bed. I'll see you tomorrow. The boys were very good and are both fast asleep." I washed my face and I went to bed. I left the light on and waited. Alf came in about one o'clock in the morning. He came right upstairs.

"Marg?" he came in the room. "I'm sorry. I went to Dora's to see what was the matter." She lived in Fazakerley. He said that she thought that it would be nice for us to have a night on our own. I jumped out of bed and got hold of a short leather razor strap and beat him around the head and shoulders with it.

"How could you treat me this way?" I shouted. "How dare you treat me this way!" Then I stopped. He never raised a hand to me.

"I deserved that," he said quietly. "Are we quite now?" I nodded my head. We were quits.

Not long after this Alf moved out. He gave me grounds for divorce and in 1946 I divorced him. He went down south with Dora. He got a job in a hotel at Falmouth as a wine waiter and she was a chambermaid at the same hotel. I think they got married down there. After a couple of years, they came back to Liverpool and bought a very nice house in Bankfield Drive. They have a son called Ronnie.

*   *   *

I made friends with a very nice Jewish girl named Gwladys. She and her husband, Ralph, owned a small gown-shop just a few minutes away from where I lived. We had a lot in common with me having been in the gown business most of my life. They had a son, Malcolm who was about Colin's age. Nearly every Sunday we would make sandwiches, prepare flasks and go in Ralph's van to Hoylake.

The sands were lovely. The three boys would scamper off to the water and we would relax in the deckchairs. There was always a large contingent of Jewish people who went to Hoylake on a Sunday. Everyone seemed to know everyone else and it was all very friendly.

When we arrived on one Sunday Colin put on his swimming trunks and I put a little pair of briefs on Dave which his Auntie Lol had knitted for him out of different coloured wool. They went off to play in the little pools left by the sea. A little later, Gwladys cried out.

"Good God, Marg! Look at your Dave!" The poor little lad was coming towards us, his legs wide apart, shuffling as if he had done something in his pants.

"Mum!" he sobbed. "Look at my pants!" His new knitted trunks were down to his ankles. The water had stretched them. He looked so funny I had to laugh, but I soon comforted him. After changing him, off he went for an ice-cream.

Another Sunday, my Aunt Agnes came and said that she was going to take us out to Moreton for the day. She said it was her treat. She loved children and was very good-hearted. It was a very hot day so I put cool little shirts and trunks on the boys. I just had on a light summer dress. Auntie had on a dark navy and white dress. It was quite pleasant but she also put on a thick black knitted cardigan. We got the train to Moreton. The place was crowded and we never saw the shore.

"I don't like it here," Colin said as soon as we got there. I told him to hush. There were dozens of stalls, hoop-la, coconut shies and racing horses and little bobby-horses which Dave went on. Colin was wailing.

"I want to go to Hoylake!" Colin wailed. Auntie was enjoying herself and going on heaps of things. She won a big black pan which she carried under her arm as there were no bags to put it in. After having a cup of tea at a stall and the boys had had an ice-cream, she turned to Colin.

"Come on then," she told him, "we'll go to Goylake." I nearly died. By now we were all a bit dishevelled. How could I face my fine friends, looking as we did? But we went. Marching along the Hoylake Prom, Auntie proudly carried her pan while I trailed along carrying her heavy cardigan as well as a few other daft prizes. The boys had their buckets and spades and balloons. Gwladys was so kind. She got out deckchairs. I was tired out and Auntie must have been exhausted, but after a nice cup of tea, we all felt much better.

"We must do this again some time," said Auntie.

CHAPTER FIVE

1945–1959

THE POST-WAR YEARS

I was very lucky to get a job in County Road as a manageress of a lovely large gown shop on the corner of Eton Street, just near Everton Football Club. I used to travel on the same bus as some of the footballers every morning. They were such fun. They used to make a playful dash to sit by me. This was good and did a lot for my fragile ego which I needed. Colin and Dave went to Anfield Road School and Mum was always there for them when they arrived home at four o'clock. She gave them their tea and stayed with them until I got home about two hours later. The boys absolutely adored her. She was a wonderful grandmother, so kind and generous with her love. She lived in a tiny four-roomed house not too far away from me. Lol lived with her while her husband was in the army.

I loved working in the gown shop. There were only two of us, Mrs Rivlin, who was about sixty years of age, was a Polish Jewess. The shop was quite large and had two fitting rooms. There were rails of dresses, coats, costumes and wedding outfits. Along one wall were wardrobes with mirrors, but the doors were always locked. One day I suggested that we use the wardrobes for all the bridal outfits. Mrs Rivlin said that they were full of old dresses from years ago and the doors hadn't been open for years. It was the time when clothes were rationed. Everybody was given so many coupons and when they ran out, you couldn't buy anything until the next issue of coupons, even if you had the money. So business wasn't too brisk. However, the keys were found and the wardrobes were opened. What a sight met our eyes. Old, very dirty but beautiful beaded dresses from about 1920 hung there, dozens of them. Chiffons, silks, satins and short skirts with long points. They were very, very dirty, but the materials hadn't deteriorated in any way. I was very enthusiastic.

"Mrs Rivlin," I said, "they are a sell." She was very pessimistic.

"They won't go," she said. She looked at my face. "Vell, my dear. Do vot you vant."

I cleared the two large windows of the garments in them and put "Big Sale, Starts Thursday 9 o'clock" notices up. Then, all Wednesday, I displayed the dresses, dozens of them. Dresses 10/- each. I wanted to charge 1, but Mrs Rivlin said no. Before we parted on Wednesday I said that we had better be early tomorrow morning as there will be a queue. Mrs Rivlin didn't think that we would sell any.

When I arrived next morning even I was astounded. The queue reached all the way to Spellow Lane about four roads away. Poor Mrs Rivlin was shaking.

"Don't worry," I said, "we will let four in at a time and only one dress each."

Of course no coupons were needed for these dresses. After two hours we had sold every one and made a lot of people very happy. We sat down to a well deserved cup of tea.

One night, when I got home from work, I sat down with Mum.

"Why don't you have a night out?" she said. "I will stay with the boys. You never go out." I wasn't very keen really but thought well why not? When I left the house I had no idea that I would finish up at The Grafton on West Derby Road, which was a very popular dance hall. I was sitting watching the happy couples dancing when I heard a lovely Scottish voice.

"You look as lonely as I feel."

I looked around and there was a sailor with the loveliest eyes one ever saw. We danced. We had lemonade. I really enjoyed myself. Mac saw me home and he made a date to go to the pictures the next time his ship docked in Liverpool. He wrote to me and we did keep our picture date. It wasn't much of a film. It was about birdwatchers and was called *The Tawny Pippet*, but we enjoyed each other's company. We saw each other quite a lot and the boys liked him. As well as the bananas that he brought back, which in the war years were almost unknown, he brought me nylons and little goodies for Mum which we couldn't get. Mum thought that he was a lovely lad. He would meet me at the shop and bring me home. Both Mr and Mrs Rivlin liked him very much. Sometimes though he was away quite a long time.

He was torpedoed three times. The last time was the worst. It was in December 1944 in the Irish Sea when the frigate HMS *Bullen* was hit by a torpedo. Half the people Mac knew drowned. Others were hanging onto the ropes of the rafts waiting to be picked up. Mac was in the water for three hours, just hanging on. He saw his shipmates dropping off one by one. His friend said, "If I don't make it and you do, will you go and see my mum?" Mac promised that he would. A bit later his buddy let go of the rope. The cold water was just too much for the poor lad. Mac was just on his last gasp when a Norwegian freighter picked him up. He didn't remember being hauled aboard but when he woke up they had stripped him of his wet clothes and wrapped him in a big blanket.

I was courting Mac at the time. He wrote to me from Chatham saying he was on ten days leave and would call and see me on his way to Scotland. This was ten days after the sinking of the *Bullen*. He had been taken to Chatham, rigged out with new clothes, been medically examined and given leave. He looked really ill. His face was very white and he had aged about ten years. He was going home for a few days rest, but first he was going to see his friend's mum who lived near Glasgow. This he did, arriving just half an hour after she had received a telegram from the War Office saying her son had died. Poor Mac said that she was in an awful state. He did his best to comfort her.

There were happier times in the Royal Navy when Mac returned. He was put on the aircraft carrier HMS *Triumph*. One day the Queen and the two princesses, Elizabeth and Margaret, visited the carrier. Some of the men took photographs and gave Mac one. He was astounded at how small the princesses were.

We married about two years later. Then Mac had to go to Malta for two years. After that he returned to "civvy street" and we were a family once again.

During Mac's later years he was very pleased to be contacted by some of the crew of the *Bullen*. They all met in 1988 and had a reunion. For the first couple of years it was held in Gorleston, near Great Yarmouth, but now the venue has come north to Lytham St Anne's. The wives of the men were also invited. Although Mac is no longer here, I still go. Gerry Marsden's father Fred was on the *Bullen* with Mac as a telephonist. Sadly, he died in 1996 and I don't know whether his wife Mary will continue going. I know that she will miss Fred very much. Steve Keeler who now runs the re-unions kindly keeps me informed of all that is happening.

I continued work at the shop. One afternoon, a lady came in. I was serving a customer, so was very surprised when Mrs Rivlin came to me and asked me to see the next customer as well. Then she walked into the backroom. I knew the customer wasn't English. When they had gone, I went into the backroom. Poor Mrs Rivlin was sitting there with the tears rolling down her cheeks.

"I couldn't serve her," she said. "She is German." Then she took a photograph from her bag and showed it to me. It was the last one she had received from Poland, taken a few years back. It showed her aged parents, three sisters and their husbands and about eight children, taken at a family gathering.

"They are all gone!" she sobbed, "in the ovens at Auschwitz. I couldn't serve her." What could I say? Words were inadequate. I put my arms round her and my sorrow joined hers. I hope it helped.

* * *

The boys were growing up quickly, so to help out I took a lodger. He was in the merchant navy, studying for his captain's ticket. He was very good-looking. I admit I fell in love with him and he likewise with me, but unfortunately he didn't believe in marriage. This was no good to me. What security had I for my two boys? His brother, Vic, used to come most weekends. Their home was in Matlock, Derbyshire.

"He loves you, Margery," he told me, "but he loves his

freedom more." So once his exams were over, I waved him bye-bye.

Mac rejoined his unit and continued to come. He was always very welcome. He asked me time and time again to marry him and I always said no. I think that I was a bit afraid. I liked him very much but I didn't love him and I didn't think it would be fair to him. "I will make you love me Marg," he would say. One weekend, when his ship was docked in Liverpool, he arrived with the news that in three weeks he was going to Malta for two years and that if I changed my mind about marrying him, just send him a telegram. Mr and Mrs Rivlin have no idea how their advice influenced my future life.

"Don't know why you don't marry that nice boy," she would say.

"You can always trust a Scotsman," Mr Rivlin said. "I am a businessman and with all my dealings with the Scots, I have never been let down." I sent the telegram.

"I'll marry you. Please send me £25. Love Marg.'

His captain gave Mac nine days leave. He dashed home and arranged everything. We were married and had four lovely days in London. We stayed at the Strand Palace Hotel. Mac had to put down a £5 deposit when we arrived there. It was very posh. The bedroom was all pink: washbasin, towels, telephone etc. I was very impressed. We rang for breakfast in bed. We stayed for four nights and saw a show each night and all the places of interest during the day. The time went so quickly. When it was time to leave, Mac went to reception to pay for the extras we had had, and he couldn't believe it when he was handed change. For four nights stay with bed and breakfast was only £4-6-8d.

On our way home, Mac suggested going into a photographer's to have our photograph taken. We found one and in we went. One entering the room, there on a stand was a Roliflex camera.

"Oh!" I said to the photographer, "my husband has one of those." He turned to Mac.

"Are you interested in photography, sir?"

"Oh!" I burst out, "not this one – the other one!" You should have seen his face. As it happened, it proved to be quite a topic of conversation in the future. I think Mac enjoyed telling the story.

Forty years later, just before our Ruby Wedding Anniversary, I sent the same bill to the Strand Palace Hotel in London. They were very impressed, took a photograph of the bill for their memorabilia file and invited Mac and I to go there for the same amount we had paid all those years ago. Champagne, flowers and fruit were all on the house. We had a lovely time.

We all felt sad when the time came for Mac to return from his leave.

"Look after your mum, boys. I will write to you everyday, dear," he said. And this he did for two years. He wrote every day. He never missed. Although his base was in Malta, he went to lots of different places and his letters were always interesting.

I had an allotment now from Mac, thirty shillings a week from Alf and my job as well, so I had no need to take in any more lodgers but one day I went into a chandlers' shop in Townsend Lane and the owner asked me if I knew anyone who would put up a young married couple. She said it was her brother and his wife. They had just had a baby and had to get out of their digs as the landlady didn't want any children. I wasn't very keen, but I felt sorry for them. I asked them to come and see me. I said they could live in the front sitting room and have the middle bedroom to sleep in and, of course, use the back kitchen for cooking. I only charged them a nominal rent.

Margery, aged two, 1915.

My husband, Mac, aged two.

*Nana Heaton, Uncle Bridges, Auntie Clara
and a little girl friend.*

Me in the Isle of Man, aged 18.

My father (marked with x)

Auntie Clara, Dad's sister.

Auntie Gertie Heaton, Dad's sister.

A family group. Mother, Lol, me and Colin.

Playing cards on our way to the Ise of Man.

Singing hymns at Kirk Bradden, 1961.
(I am in the centre of the front row).

Our Bowling team in the Isle of Man, 1961.
(I am on the front row, second from the right).

Taken on a days outing with our Bowling team.
(I am fifth from the right. My daughter, Sandra,
is on the front row, the tallest little girl).

1971 Winners at New Brighton Bowls Tournament.

I could see that they were not very well off, but one thing that I did do was to get them to sign a paper saying that they would leave when Mac came home.

How sorry I was that I let them come. At first they seemed all right but then, as the baby became older, they became lazy and dirty. Often, when Mum came, she said they had gone out and left the electric fire on. When I told them to be more considerate they would be nasty to me. I went into their room once with a letter for them. I knocked on the door and she said "come in". She was holding the baby over my tiled hearth to do its business, no potty at all.

*   *   *

At last, Mac was coming home. How glad I was to hear this. I told them that they had to go. They didn't want to go but I said that I had the signed agreement saying that they would leave when Mac returned. They left two days before Mac arrived. I had to put a new fireplace in the room they were in because it was the only way of getting rid of the stench.

It was great having Mac home. He helped with the boys. As well as a bit of discipline which they needed, he also showed an interest in their well-being. He took them to the speedway and the motorbike racing which they loved. He also took them to cinema. On the whole, life was quite good. Mac had been in the Royal Navy for seventeen years altogether. We married just over two years before he finished. If he had stayed another 4 years, he would have got a pension, but as he said, "it's a great life for a single bloke, but no life for a happily married man." I loved having him home.

He told me so many tales of things that he had seen and done. One of the most poignant was a mission that he wished he could forget but, being part of the Royal Navy, he had to do as he was told. Soon after the war, the Jews were going back to Palestine, their promised land. There were thousands of them, filling any ship that would take them, packed like sardines. They were in a pitiful state. The Royal Navy were told to let no more ships into Haifa Harbour. They had to board the ships and make them turn around and go back. The Jews refused. Mac was one of the boarding party. He said the women had long pointed needles and they were sticking them into the sailors as they climbed over the ship's rail. Who can blame them? I've long been an admirer of the Jewish race. They have suffered so much and, after all, the land had been given to them, but I guess that their timing was wrong. They should have extended Palestine gradually, a few at a time. Instead, hundreds drowned and died of disease and starvation. Mac said that the smell and condition of the ship was deplorable. He was glad when the Jews finally won and were allowed to embark.

His first job after leaving the navy was on the buses, but the split duties and uneven hours were getting him down. He became a bank messenger and then a security man with regular hours, which was much better for everyone.

On July 6th 1951, I gave birth to a lovely daughter. We called her Sandra. We were all delighted. We were now a complete little family. My only blackspot was Mac's mum. She died six months before Sandra was born. I felt so very sad that she never ever saw her granddaughter. The boys loved Sandra. They treated her like a big doll. Dave was now ten and Colin was twelve. They were a great help to me and she was a very good, happy baby. Mac would walk around the room with her singing, "A Gordon for Me". We were a happy family.

Mum still lived in her little house in Wilmer Road. We saw each other almost every day but I think she must have felt a bit lonely. Lol had gone to live in Birmingham as her husband had got a job there. One day, Mum told me that my Uncle Bridger had called to see her. He had married my dad's sister Clara, but my Aunt Clara had died six years earlier. He called on my Mum quite a lot after his first visit. I never liked him. He was brash and full of himself. I must admit that he had done a lot with his life. He had been in the 1914–18 war and had been a mercenary in the Anglo-Irish war of 1921 and had been in the Black and Tans. The last was he was involved in was as a cavalryman during the Spanish Civil War.

One Monday morning, Mum and Uncle Bridger called. I was busy washing clothes. They sat down.

"Tell her girl!" he said to Mum. She looked at me.

"Bridger has asked me to marry him," she said.

"What?" I jumped out of my chair. "But Mum, you never liked him," I spluttered.

"Well," Mum said quietly, "we are both on our own and we would be company for each other." They were married. Both Lol and I were against it but gave Mum our blessing. She moved into my uncle's house in Fazakerley. It had a nice garden and she seemed quite happy at first. Then her health deteriorated and she died two years later.

The day of the funeral poor Dave cried and cried. We had Mum buried with Dad. Uncle wasn't too pleased, but Lol and I thought it was only right. I was devastated. My dear mum gone. I went out. The sun shone, the sky was so blue, the tree's so green, people were walking along talking and laughing. "How can they feel like this?" I thought. To me, the world was different. These thoughts remained with me for a long time.

Colin had gone quite well at school, but his passion was art. At fourteen he passed an exam for the College of Art. By the time he was sixteen he had passed his first diploma. He then said that he couldn't take his degree until he was eighteen and as he was more or less just wasting his time at the College, he said that there was nothing more they could teach him. In fact, he was himself helping to teach the newcomers. He decided to spread his wings and took off to London.

Dave was a very happy-go-lucky little boy. He didn't like school at all, he couldn't care less whether he got good marks or not. Mac and I used to despair.

"But Dave, what will you do when you leave school?"

"I want to go to sea," was his reply. With that in mind, the same day that he left school at four o'clock, he started work at six, at the best hotel in Liverpool, the Adelphi, to train to be a waiter. He stayed there until he was seventeen when he joined the Cunard Shipping Company as a first class waiter.

Now Bridger was on his own I would go once a week to do his shopping, although I didn't like him much. I did it mainly for Mother's sake. He came every Sunday and had dinner with us. Poor Mac had to suffer his smelly pipe. He would talk about all his soldiering days, and there were many, believe me! I think that he enjoyed all these skirmishes. He was certainly very tough. He would roar with laughter at some of the things he had done. He said one night in Ireland he was walking through the thick undergrowth and saw this big rat, so he shot it. The next second, he said, this old biddy who had been sitting in an outdoor privy came screaming out through the door with her bloomers around her ankles. She thought she was being attacked.

One Sunday when he came he was telling us that the night previous after his bath he had put his radio in the water and given it a good wash. He said that it was very dirty. Then he dried it off a bit and put it in the oven for a while. He had a Triplex fire oven. I was aghast at this.

"Oh my! – does it go?" I asked. He just roared laughing. "Does it hell!" he said. Next week he came round and took his coat off.

"What do you think, girl?" he asked, "I put the pantry light on and the bloody radio came on! Its great now, better than ever."

One day, the police came to tell me that the postman had found Uncle lying on the garden path. He had called an ambulance and that Uncle was now in Walton Hospital. I quickly put my coat on, left word for Mac who was at work and off I went. I expected to see a very sick old man, but not on your life. He was sitting up in bed, looking quite bright and cheerful.

"What happened?" I asked.

"I don't know," he replied, "but an ambulance came and two men wanted to put me on a stretcher. I told them I wasn't getting on that thing!" They persuaded him to go in a chair and then wrapped a big red blanket around him. "I felt like Father bloody Christmas!" he said.

"Oh Uncle," I said and laughed, "well, there doesn't seem to be much wrong with you."

I looked around the big ward. There seemed to be quite a number of very ill- looking men. It was just about three o'clock and the nurse was just opening the doors of the ward to let the visitors in. Uncle Bridger, in a very loud voice, shouted out.

"Into the valley of death rode the six hundred". I felt that I could have died with shame. Nurse came and told him to be quiet.

Uncle had lots of tests and proved to be quite a nuisance really. He was put in a cot bed. He was always trying to climb out. It was decided that he couldn't go home again to live on his own, so he was transferred to the John Bagat Nursing

Home. This was quite near to where I lived and I often went to see him. He seemed quite happy there. He thought that he was in the Isle of Man.

"Look girl," he would say, looking out of the window, "there's Douglas Head."

All of the staff there liked him. He made them laugh and I understood what they meant. However, Uncle got thinner and thinner and eventually he just passed quietly away.

He left Lol and I a small endowment each, about £65. The rest of his goods and money he left to this lady who lived in the Isle of Man. It seems that years ago her mother was the bridesmaid when he had married Clara. He had always kept in touch with the family. I wrote to Miss Robert's and told her of Uncle's death. I received a very nice letter from her saying that she and her brother would come to Uncle Bridger's cremation.

On the day, there were only the six of us there. Miss Roberts and her brother, Lol and Charl, and Mac and I. A young minister took the service and after prayers and a short address, he began the Committal,

"We are here today to put to rest our dear sister Bridget". I listened, horrorstruck. I think that we were all dumb with shock. The minister carried on. We didn't know what to do. Then it was too late. "We now commit her body to the deep". The curtains closed. My loud, egotistical, brave, rumbustious uncle had been buried a woman! We shook hands with the young minister and didn't say anything. Then we looked at each other.

"Well," said Miss Roberts, "if he knows anything about this, I bet he's laughing his head off!"

Mac and I never stopped the boys from seeing their father. In fact we all became friends and visited each others houses. I used to look on Alf as a relative in some way. I liked and got on well with Dora. I often wonder at my attitude in this situation. I knew that I no longer loved Alf and my dear Mac used to say "I've a lot to thank him for. If he hadn't met Dora, I'd never have had you." Wasn't that fantastic of him? All I knew was that I had great peace of mind.

With the boys off my hands and Sandra settled at Holy Trinity Church School, a neighbour, Mrs Smith, asked me to join the bowling club that she belonged to. The green was only five minutes away. This I did and it proved to be one of the finest pastimes that I ever undertook.

I hadn't been in the bowling club long when I learned that they were going to the Isle of Man to enter the ladies bowling competition which was held every year. Most of the clubs in Liverpool and Merseyside entered. Our club went under the name of Oakfield Ladies. Mac became very interested in the bowling and encouraged me no end. When I was asked if I would go with them, he wasn't a bit put out.

"You go dear. Sandra and Dave will be all right with me."

Off I went for a week. The boat fare and full board was £7/10/0d inclusive. I think thirteen of our club went that year. I enjoyed the sea journey, but a few of the ladies were a little apprehensive. However, the sea was quite calm. We stayed on the top deck and played cards. I just loved entering Douglas Harbour: the big sweep of the bay, the golden sands, Douglas Head with the lighthouse and the lovely green hills. I had been a couple of times previously with Lol when I was a teenager. We stayed at the house of a friend of my aunts', near the Villa Marina. She was a lovely old lady who had a wooden leg.

Mrs Senegles, the old lady, had a daughter called Carrie. We became great friends, although she must have been about thirty. She was the warden at the woman's prison near Douglas. One day I asked her if she got many awkward prisoners.

"At the moment," she replied, "we haven't got anyone in. I think the last one in was about six weeks ago. I just sit and knit. It's very boring. We don't get much crime here!"

It was Monday morning and the first day of the competition. It was held on the bowling green of the Villa Marina. It was full of spectators sitting on the rows of seats around the green. I felt very nervous.

"You'll be all right, Mac," my friends said, "it will be an experience for you."

My name was eventually called out. My opponent was someone from West Kirby. She looked very efficient and very tall. I'm only 4ft 11in. Anyway, we started off. My first wood was very short, only halfway up the green. She bowled her first wood. It was about a foot away from the jack, a good wood. I stood on the mat, took a deep breath and bowled my second wood. It fell about a foot away from the jack, the other side.

"Who's in?" she asked me.

"I can't tell from here," I said, "shall I go and have a look."

"If you will," she replied.

I walked up towards the end. On the way, I picked up my very short wood which I had bowled. I got to the jack and was looking at who was nearest.

"I can't tell," I shouted back at her, "it's a measure."

"Measure," she called.

"You haven't sent your other wood yet," shouted the referee. The referee came marching up the green. "What did you pick up your wood for?" she asked. I looked at her.

"I thought that it would be in her way," I said. How everyone laughed. It was hilarious. She patted my shoulder. I think that she realised then that I was only a "raw recruit". Of course, I didn't win my first match, but I enjoyed it.

We had many wonderful times with the bowling club. I was

in Oakfield Ladies for about twenty years. I was never an exceptional bowler, but I did win a few prizes. Two of our ladies were county bowlers. One of them, Doris Sleeman, I reckon, the best bowler in Liverpool. She is my friend to this day. We are the only two alive now out of our original team.

Another episode in my bowling days that I feel that I must not leave out was when our club decided to have a day out and play for our cup on a neutral green. We set off for a very nice country pub which had a bowling green at the back. It was a knockout competition. We all played each other until only two were left. We had a lovely day, a very good meal and then who should be in the final, but Doris and myself. It was a very good game. We were 20-20. It all depended on the last end. We played and we both walked up the green. I looked. I couldn't believe it. I was nearest the jack, but it was a close thing, I must admit. Doris looked and shouted for measures. Mr Smith, one of our members husbands came up with the pegs as we called them. He looked at the end.

"I like that," he said pointing to my wood. Of course, he didn't know which was which. Doris took the pegs off him as he went to peg.

"Outsiders can't peg," she said. She bent down and pegged herself in.

"I'm in."

She put her hand up. Everybody clapped and we shook hands. I was bitterly disappointed, but not because of losing.

The same competition came two years later and I was playing Doris again in the final for the same cup. It was another good match and we were 20 across. Then we came to the last end. We walked up the green together. I looked and I wasn't in I knew. Doris looked, then quickly kicked the woods in and held up my hand.

"Mac's won!" she shouted. Everybody clapped. My eyes were shining with unshed tears. I felt that I hadn't won the match, but I had won my friend.

Every year, all the lady bowlers of Liverpool held an annual dance. After a lovely meal there was a talent competition. Every club could enter if they wished. I used to write all the scripts for our club. Some of our members were quite stout, others tall and very slim. Can you imagine us as fairies? We were hilarious. The next year we went as sportsmen and women. The next year we went as beauty queens with very little on, heavy make-up, very high heels, wigs and beauty spots. Nobody could match our talent. We won three times in succession.

At our fourth attempt we came second, but that year we couldn't put our heart into things. We lost one of our dearest friends, Marjorie Boughton. She died of a brain hemorrhage very suddenly. The evening before, Doris, myself, Marg and Netta, who was Margie's sister, were playing solo whist. The next night, Marg was dead. Doris never seemed the same after that. She thought the world of Marg. She even gave up bowling for a time. I felt very sad also. Although I saw Marg quite a lot, I seemed to get over the loss quicker than Doris. Previous to this, Doris lost her sister-in-law with a tumour on the brain. She was also in our team and was a very good bowler. So this was the second loss she had had to suffer. She retired into herself for quite a while and didn't want to take part in anything. She would only go out with George, her very devoted husband. The next summer she returned to her bowling.

We would go to the bingo a couple of times a week and both enjoyed it. Some times we had a win, but we always shared them. When I got home I would give half of my winnings to Mac.

"Good for you, hen," he would say. When I came home losing, he would laughingly say, "You're a load of rubbish!"

Some of the happiest years of my life were spent with the Oakfield Ladies Bowling Team. We were in a league and played other teams, entered competitions, went to various towns, seaside places and what have you. During the winter months, we went to whist-drives at each others houses. Mac never minded me doing this. He was interested in all I did. His love was football. He liked all the sports on television.

Coming home from my shopping one very sunny afternoon, a little bird settled on my shoulder. I looked sideways. It was a budgerigar. I was only a few steps from home. I went up my path and opened the front door. It still sat on my shoulder. When I went into my living room, he flew onto the back of the chair.

"Hello, Sparky!" he said. I was enchanted. He was lovely. I could see that he had been well looked after. I found a cage which I had from a canary which Dave had bought for me a few years ago. I put him in this for the time being. After I'd had my lunch, I wrote a statement, "Bird Found" etc. I knew that someone would be pining for their lost pet. I then went to the pet store and asked them to put the statement in the front of the window. Of course, I then bought some food for my little lodger. Days passed and I had no enquiries. I put more notices in various shops. Still no replies. I realised then that my little bird had come to stay.

What a clever little pal he turned out to be. He would recite many nursery rhymes: Georgie Porgie Pudding and Pie, Little Miss Muffet and Jack and Jill. He was a wonderful talker and we all grew to love him.

About four years later I was having a whist-drive for members of the bowling club. There were a couple of new members who had joined the club, but who had never been to my house before. One of those was a Mrs Sally Roberts. We had the whist-drive and settled down to refreshments. Suddenly, my bird, who had been very quiet, said very clearly, "Hello Sparky". Mrs Roberts looked up.

"That's my daughter's bird!" she said. "She lost it about four years ago." I didn't know what to say. I then told her how I had tried to find the owner. She was very nice. She said that her daughter would be so very pleased to hear that he had found such a good home, that she had another bird now and wouldn't want to take Sparky off me. My little pal lived quite a few years more and gave us so much pleasure.

We woke up one Bank Holiday morning to find the sun shining. The sky was so blue that we could tell it was going to be a fantastic day.

"Can't we go out for the day?" asked Sandra. She was about seven at the time.

"Yes," I said, "lets go to Rhyl." Mac demurred.

"I never like going out on Bank Holidays. Too many crowds." We looked so crestfallen. He looked at our faces. "Oh well, all right, but we're not staying late."

We left the house about ten o'clock to get a bus to the station but they all went sailing past, full-up.

"This is hopeless," said Mac after about twenty minutes. "Come on across the road and we'll get one going in the opposite way and when it turns around to come back, we will stay on."

This we did and eventually we arrived at the station. The train was full as expected. When we arrived at Rhyl I think that all the northwest region had decided to go as well. It was overflowing. All of the deckchairs were taken and we had to queue up for the toilets. There were endless queues for ice-creams. It was so hot. We wandered around and I felt worn out.

"Shall we find a café and have something to eat?" I suggested. "I'm dying for a cup of tea."

We found one and after about twenty minutes wait the three of us were ushered to a table. I was glad to sit down. We sat and sat. No-one came near us. They were very busy, I must admit. Mac said to a passing waitress.

"Miss!"

"Just a moment, Sir!" she said and passed on. After a while, Mac got up and went to another waitress. His Scottish temper was rising.

"Excuse me, but who is the waitress for our table?"

"Oh," was the reply, "she's gone off but another one is coming on!" We sat and sat. People who had come into the cafe long after us had eaten and gone. At last, Mac could bear it no longer.

"Come on," he said, "we're going!" When we reached the door beside the cash desk, the cashier stopped us.

"Have you got your bill, sir?" I think that was the straw that broke the camel's back.

"What?" roared Mac, "what?" In a deadly cold voice, he continued. "We've been here long enough to have eaten three dinners, but we haven't had one cup of tea! Don't you dare ask me for the bill!" He stormed out. Poor Sandra and I followed him. We walked along the promenade.

"Well, we did have a sit-down," I said meekly. It was now nearly five o'clock.

"Let's get an early train and go home," said Mac. So we made our way to the station. When we arrived there the platform was fairly empty, but when the train arrived at half-five it was teaming with people, all deciding to get home early.

"Now," said Mac, "San and I will push on first and get a seat and you try and get on as fast as you can." He knew that I wasn't the pushing type. The train came steaming in. Mac and Sandra were soon on the train. I struggled a little bit. There was such a crush of people. However, I was eventually mounting the steps of the train when it happened. My shoe fell off! I looked down. It lay on the railway line. Oh dear! I got on hesitatingly. There was Mac and Sandra sitting down. Mac looked at my face.

"What's the matter?" he asked.

"I've lost my shoe!" I whispered.

"What do you mean, Marg, you've lost your shoe?"

"It dropped off. It's on the railway line."

"Bloody hell!" he said. He stood up.

"It doesn't matter," I said.

"What do you mean, 'it doesn't matter'. How can you walk home."

"I can hop!" I said.

"Get off, you silly bitch!"

We all got off the train. Mac found a porter who retrieved the shoe with a long hook. Mac gave him 5/-. By now, you couldn't even get on the train. People were standing tightly together.

"Come with me," the porter said and he allowed us to travel in the luggage van. I looked at Sandra, then I looked at Mac very dolefully. He looked at us both, then he laughed and laughed.

"Don't ask me to take you out on any more Bank Holidays," he said. What a man!

*   *   *

1959 proved to be quite a momentous year. Dave was doing quite well in the merchant navy with the Cunard Shipping Company. Colin was in London doing very well at his art, architectural design and murals. He did quite a number of things, always learning and teaching himself through experience.

One weekend, when Dave was home from sea, he asked me if he could bring a girl home for tea.

"Of course you can," I replied. She lived in Wallasey. When she arrived, I could see why Dave was so smitten, for indeed she was lovely. A real English beauty with lovely blond hair, fair complexion and big blue eyes.

"This is Bet, Mum," he said. He followed me into the kitchen where I was preparing the meal.

"Isn't she lovely, Mum?" he kept saying.

"Yes, Dave, she's lovely," I replied. I went on with the meal. He came in again.

"You do like her, don't you, Mum?"

"Yes, Dave, I like her." Yet again he came in.

"Isn't she beautiful, Mum?" I looked at him.

"I think she's lovely! She's beautiful! I like her! Now will you go and sit at the table. Tea is ready." Colin wrote to me from London saying that he had met a lovely Phillipino girl and that he was bringing her home to meet me. He also said that they were to be accompanied by her sister, who has to chaperone her as they are not allowed to be on their own until they were married. It was apparently their custom.

Colin arrived with Nolita and Anya. She was also beautiful. She had long black hair, lovely big brown eyes and rather full lips. She spoke English very well and had been well educated. Her father worked at the Phillipino embassy with the ambassador. She and her sisters had been presented to the Queen Mary at the last court held. Colin told me that they hoped to marry in May or June.

One Saturday, Dave was returning to the ship after his weekend at home. I'll always remember his face. It was just glowing.

"I'm so happy, Mum!" he said, as he kissed me good-bye.

The next day, Sunday, Mac, Sandra and I were just relaxing after our dinner when there was a knock on the front door. I went and opened it. There on the doorstep was Betty, her mum and her sister, Maureen.

"Come in," I said, taking them into the sitting room, "please sit down."

"Well,' said her mum, "it's not very pleasant news I bring. Bet's pregnant." I looked at them. I was stunned.

"It's not Dave's fault," said Bet, "I made him."

"Well," I said, "it takes two." I sat for a few minutes. Then I asked Mac to make us a cup of tea. It was the first time that I had seen Bet's mum and I liked her immediately. Mac came in with the tea and Bet introduced him to her mum and to Maureen.

"Well," said Mrs Randle, "Bet's a good girl and her dad says that she's going to be married in white and have a proper do, reception, the lot and he will pay for it all."

"That's very good of him," I said, "but I must help too."

In three weeks, when Dave was due home, everything had been arranged: the vicar, the room for the reception, the invitations sent out etc. When Dave came home, he was ecstatic.

"We do love each other, Mum!"

It was a lovely wedding. Betty looked beautiful in her long white gown. I made Sandra a very pretty dress in primrose yellow. She made a lovely little bridesmaid. Bet's sister, Maureen, was the chief bridesmaid and she looked nice also. On the day, everything went so well. You wouldn't have thought that it only took barely a month to organise.

Dave and Bet have now been happily married for thirty seven years.

Colin married Nolita a month after Dave was married to Bet. It was a lovely wedding. The reception was held at the Phillipino Embassy. Two princesses and the ex-King of Nepal were there. It was the very first Phillipino wedding in London. The reporters were there and next morning it was in all the London papers. The marriage lasted for twenty five years, then there was a divorce and each went their separate ways. They had two lovely children, Marisol and Jason.

In 1990, Colin married a lovely Japanese girl called, Tamea. Nolita now has a boyfriend and lives in Malta.

CHAPTER SIX

1960–1986

SEDLEY STREET

During the war, Sedley Street, the road next to Richmond Park, was bombed. Nine houses on one side of the street were demolished. In 1952, new houses were built in their place, but instead of building nine, the builders only put up seven. They had a nice hall, an upstairs bathroom, two bedrooms and a lovely long living room and who should buy one but my dear friend Prim, who used to wheel David in his pram. She was married now with a little girl called Margaret. She and Sandra became great friends. Of course I was highly delighted. We saw each other almost every day. We were such friends and I loved her wee house. It was always so bright and sunny.

"Prim, if you ever leave your little house, will you sell it to me?" I asked at one of our coffee mornings.

"Of course I will,' she replied.

Eight years later she kept her promise. She was moving to Ellesmere Port. Sandra was nine at the time. Poor Prim had been having difficulties with her marriage. I knew that I would greatly miss her. We would always remain friends and still are to this day.

When we bought the house in Sedley Street, Mac and I had very little money. We needed £200 for a deposit, which we hadn't got. Lol lent me £100 and my aunt lent me £100. I managed to get a job in a gown shop at 3 shillings an hour doing alterations. In twelve months I'd paid back all that I had borrowed. I continued to work at that shop for sixteen years. When I left, all I got was £10 holiday money.

Sandra was quite a clever girl. She passed her Eleven Plus exam and went to Holly Lodge Grammar School. She was there until she was eighteen, when she went to University. When she was eleven, we bought her a Siamese cat. She called her Tu-Chin. She was lovely and so clever. We all adored her. In those days, I used to have a clothes rack on which I would put the clothes when they had been washed. To dry them we had to draw it up to the ceiling using a pulley. Often Sandra would call down from upstairs.

"Mum, can I have my tights." As soon as Tu-Chin heard her voice, no matter where she was, she would race and sit at the bottom of the stairs until I came and put the tights loosely around her neck and up she would trot, so proudly, to Sandra. The same happened with panties and roll-ons. It didn't matter. Whatever it was, Tu-Chin was there to deliver it and receive a kindly stroke on her head.

"There's a clever girl!"

She loved Sandra so much. One day I made her a Holly Lodge outfit, just like Sandra's, green and white striped blouse, a tie and a navy skirt. She would sit quite contentedly in a little chair in the yard with Sandra while she did her homework.

Tu-Chin lived to be eighteen and a half. We were all very upset when she died and buried her in my friend's garden.

About 1962, I went to visit Aunt Agnes. She had been in hospital with a fractured hip for about six weeks. Her husband,

Uncle George, had been looked after by his niece who went for his shopping. She lived in the same road, so it wasn't much trouble for her. She was a very nice lady. Her husband brought Auntie's bed down and put it into the parlour, for Auntie wouldn't be able to climb the stairs for quite a long time. I was pleased to see Aunt Agnes was looking quite well considering what she had been through.

After I had made her lunch and she had had a cup of tea, she leaned forward.

"Marg, will you do something for me?" she said.

"Of course," I said. Little did I realise what I was letting myself in for.

"Well," said Auntie, "the cleaner refuses to do George's bedroom and I don't like asking Ethel who does our shopping, but Uncle's shirts have flea dirt on and I know his bed wants changing. I think there are fleas in the bed, although George says that he can't feel anything. George can sleep in the middle bedroom until his room is cleaned."

My heart sank. One thing I can't stand are fleas.

"What do you want me to do Auntie." She said to fill a bucket with hot water and put some disinfectant in it. She handed me a big box of flea powder.

"Open the window and throw all the bedding out into the backyard. There's a tin bath there full of soapy water. I'll put the bedding in it. When you've done that, try and catch any fleas you can and put them into the bucket of water. Then empty the flea powder over the bed and skirting boards."

Believe me when I tell you this was one of the worst days of my life. I went upstairs with the bucket. My heart was beating quickly. I felt frightened, but I knew Auntie was worried. I opened the bedroom door which was tightly shut. I went in and shut the door quickly. I couldn't believe it. There were fleas everywhere.

They were all over the walls and the dressing table was one mass of fleas. They jumped on me. I was terrified. I opened the windows and started to throw the bedding out. Sheets, blankets, the pillowcases, which were once white, were covered red with flea-dirt and Uncle's blood. You couldn't see a bit of white. The fleas were jumping all over me, the bed and the walls. I caught as many as I could and put them in the bucket of water. I threw the flea powder everywhere. After about twenty minutes went downstairs, carrying the bucket.

"I'm going home, Auntie. I'll come tomorrow. Just get some more powder."

I went home. Mac opened the door.

"Don't come near me," I said, "I'm going to have a bath." I went straight upstairs, stripped off and got into the bath. I washed my hair and then when I got out, I just dumped my clothes in the water. I felt a lot better. There were eighteen fleas in the water. I went back the next day and washed the bed, dressing table and chairs and threw more powder around me. I went home, got bathed and dumped all my clothes in the water again.

It took four days to get rid of the fleas. Auntie was very grateful and wanted to give me a couple of pounds, which I declined. I just couldn't take any money off her. I was pleased that I had helped to relieve her mind, but I never wanted to see another flea ever again.

* * *

1969 was the year Lol, Charl, Mac and I went on holiday to Jeselo in Italy. We had a wonderful journey. We traveled by boat from Dover to Ostende, then overland by huge coaches. They were very comfortable with toilets, and marvellous sleeping arrangements. We drove through Belgium, which was very flat countryside, through France and then we travelled all night on the Autobahn arriving in Munich in time for breakfast. We didn't stay long for we still had a long way to go.

I really enjoyed the rest of the journey. We went through the little village of Oberamagau, which was very picturesque. It happened to be one of the years that they put on the Passion Play. Most of the people were dressed up as in Biblical times. The houses were newly painted with large murals of scenes from Biblical days. It was very interesting. They only perform the play every seven years, but while it is on the people dress up as they would have done if they had lived in those days so long ago. We stopped for lunch and then set off on our way again.

We passed ski slopes in Austria. When we arrived at the Austrian border, we were held up for three hours. The Austrian police came on the coach and arrested the courier. The poor girl was crying. It seems that she should have declared some whisky which was put on the coach at Ostende. This she had failed to do. This was her first job and being new she hadn't been told what to do. She should have told us to say that we had bought a bottle of whiskey each, which we were allowed to do. So when the Austrian police boarded the coach in uniform, with guns in their belts they looked very formidable and we were all asked if we had bought whiskey. Of course, we all said "No". They said that the coach could carry on, but not the courier. They confiscated the whisky. Well, the driver couldn't go without the courier. After three hours, they decided to let the courier go, but she had to pay £87 and appear in court in a week's time. We were only allowed to leave the coach to go to the toilet.

Eventually, we continued on our way. When we reached the Italian border, three hours late, the Italian driver who now took over wasn't very pleased. We still had a long way to go. The scenery was breathtaking through the Italian Alps and then the Dolomites. We were so high up in the mountains. The roads were very narrow and twisting and turning. When we looked down, we could hardly see the bottom of the valleys below. It was no wonder that an Italian driver was on this route. It would have to be someone who knew the roads well. One slip and we would have been over the top.

By now it was getting quite dark. I began to feel a bit frightened. Being in the mountains we didn't have the comfort of overhead fluorescent lighting. However, we reached our hotel at last at eleven o'clock at night. We should have arrived at eight o'clock. The lady very kindly put a meal on for us, although it was so late. I think everybody was glad to get to bed.

Next morning, we took a survey of our hotel. It wasn't very large, but we had a nice bedroom with a balcony. It was very clean. Our breakfast was very plain, but sufficient.

We walked around Jeselo and it was a lovely day. Charlie couldn't resist opening the grids of the sewers as we passed. He said he wanted to see how their water system worked. I expected a policeman to come along any minute and put a hand on his shoulder and ask him what he was up to. Poor Lol looked quite worried.

"I don't think that you should do that, Charl," she said, but he only laughed. However, no policeman came along, so we made our way down to the beach.

It was a nice beach. Plenty of deckchairs and refreshments nearby. We had only booked for breakfast and evening meal, so we could do what we liked for lunch. After a nap in a deckchair, Charl got up and wandered off. I thought he had gone to the toilet, but after two hours we were beginning to feel a bit worried. Then he strolled up with a big grin on his face.

"I've been down the sewers helping the Italians to fix a pipe," he said, quite pleased with himself.

We went back for our evening meal. It didn't impress me at all. I think that it was octopus and various vegetables, but the sweet or dessert was always a bowl of fresh fruit. This never varied. I didn't mind really. What could you expect for a package holiday for only £25 each, everything included.

One day, we went to Venice, a beautiful old town and very picturesque: the canal with the gondolas, the arches and wonderful architecture. As we went inland though I found that there was a smell from the water and I don't think that I could live there. We went to feed the pigeons in St Mark's Square and took some snaps.

On another day, Charl thought that he would like to take a trip to Yugoslavia, but the three of us just decided to laze around on the beach. With Mac having been in the navy for seventeen years, he had been to most of these places, so he just relaxed with Lol and I. I think Charl quite enjoyed his day. He had been down the salt mines.

We really enjoyed the journey back home through the lovely mountains. This time we saw them in the sunshine. We went through Cortina and saw the gun turrets in the mountains that the Italians had built during the war. We were sorry to be going home for we all had had a very enjoyable journey.

*　　*　　*

I never regretted marrying Mac. He was the dearest, kindest person I have ever known. We got on so well together. Being in the navy for so long, he was eligible to join the Corps of Commissionaires. This he did and he got a lot of pleasure out of it. Every Saturday he would be on duty at either Everton or Liverpool football matches. He just loved football, especially Everton. Other times, he would be asked to go to the big golf tournaments at Hoylake, etc. Or to go to the big races such as the Grand National and Haydock. He often went to banquets. I would go to my bowls. We never got bored with each other and always had plenty to talk about. We both loved watching sport on television, even cricket!

One Sunday, Lancashire were playing a cricket match at Old Trafford, Manchester.

"Shall we all go?" Sandra said, "it's a lovely day." She turned to me.

"No, love," I said. "You two go. It will be too hot for me. I'll make some sandwiches and you can have your dinner when you get back."

"Well, take it easy, hen," said Mac, "read the papers and have a rest." This I promised to do.

As soon as they left, I thought I would give the backyard door a coat of paint. It certainly needed it. By the time I had painted the frame and both sides, I was feeling quite tired, but also pleased with my achievement. It was now becoming quite hot. I'll sit down I thought and have a rest and look at the Sunday paper for a few minutes before I have lunch. I brought the striped upright chair out into the yard, got the paper and sat down. I immediately fell through. There I was with my backside on the floor of the yard, stuck firmly in the chair. I couldn't get out. I tried all different ways, pressing my arms on the arms of the chair, but to no avail. I was firmly stuck. Half an hour went by. It was getting very hot and I was beginning to get very worried. I tried shouting to my neighbours, Joan and Margaret, but no-one heard me. I thought, if I'm still sitting here in this great heat by six o'clock I'll be dead. I was afraid to do anything very physical for I'd had a major operation previously. However, I realised that I must do something. I slithered along the ground, got a hand on one of my large flower containers, half pulled the chair on its side and, at last, got one hip free. After that it was easy. I was so relieved.

Mac and Sandra arrived home about 6.30 pm.

"Had a nice easy day dear?" asked Mac.

When I told them what had happened, they both roared laughing. Even I could see the funny side of it, but of course they were sorry also and glad that I was all right.

*   *   *

Dave and Bet had bought a house in St Helen's. Dave left the sea and got a job in a bottle factory there, but he couldn't settle. Bet's sister came over from Canada and the next thing that we knew, they had decided to emigrate there.

It was a very big wrench for us all, but it proved to be the right thing for them to do. They now have another daughter, Lydia. They got on quite well. Dave's first house was in Stony Plain, an Indian Reservation and Lydia was born there.

At first, Dave took any job that he could get while he had a look around. Eventually he opened a restaurant with another friend. This went very well for a time, but then the recession came and he decided to sell. He now has a very good job as a sales representative and travels all over Alberta, thousands of miles every year. He is very good at his job, but it must be very tiring and also at times be very lonely for Bet. It's a good job that she has Karen and the children living so near.

When Sandra finished at Holly Lodge, she went to Manchester University, but after three months she transferred to Liverpool University. She wanted to be nearer home. She got on very well at it. She got an honours degree in Mathematics, passed her Physics and also Statistical Science of Computing. She was well set for her future. Her first job was at UCSL in Bromborough, working with computers. She hadn't been there long when she decided to buy a motorbike. I was terrified. It was a lovely new bike. She went out on her first trial run.

"It'll be all right Mum, I'll just go round Richmond Park." She wasn't out long. She had put a small dent in a neighbour's car.

"Sandra, you are not riding that bike until you have had lessons!" I stormed. So, every Sunday, she had lessons at the Birkenhead School of Motoring and every Sunday she arrived home full of bruises. After a couple more lessons, I asked how she was getting on.

"Well Mum, lets say I'm getting better at falling off." Soon after this, she sold the bike. I think she realised that it just wasn't her thing. She lost £100 on the deal, but I would have given it away for nothing.

Six months after our holiday to Italy, I had to go into hospital for a major operation. I used to go to bed propped up with about four pillows and if I slipped down during sleep I would wake up choking. I couldn't get my breath. This used to happen about three times every night. The doctor sent me to hospital for investigation. The medical consultant told me that I had a hiatus hernia. He was no advocate for surgery at all but, in my case, there was nothing for me but an operation.

He told me to go and see my doctor as he would be writing to him.

My doctor read the letter and sent for me.

"So! You don't want the operation."

"Not really," I replied.

"Well," said my doctor, "I'm going to be very blunt. If you have the operation its a 50-50 chance. If you die on the operating table, you won't know anything about it. Only those who are left will feel the hurt. But if you don't have the operation, your windpipe and your lungs will be destroyed by the acid that you are choking on and you will have a terrible death."

Dr Toke never held his punches and, of course, that talk decided me. I went to have the operation at nine o'clock on a Monday morning in January 1970. I came round at seven o'clock that night. Poor Mac was there when I woke up but he didn't stay long.

I was very ill, but after a couple of days I began to feel a bit better. I took stock of myself. I had tubes all over me and I was being fed intravenously. My mouth felt terrible and the nurses used to wipe my lips with ice.

On the fifth day, the sister came to take the drains out of my stomach. These were tubes about six inches long. They were very difficult to get out as they had been in so long. Mr Howell Hughes, the surgeon, said he wanted to make sure that the stomach was well drained.

"I'm sorry. I know it's hurting you," said the poor sister.

"It doesn't matter," I said, "do it quick!" After this procedure, she came to me with a tiny medicine glass with about a quarter of an inch of water in it.

"Now," she said, "you must only sip this very slowly." As I had had nothing pass my lips for five days, I was only too glad to do this. About three hours later, she came with another glass. This time it had about half an inch of water in it.

"Now, you must only sip it," she said. I was longing to swallow some, but I thought that I'd better not. It was tea-time now in the ward. Everybody seemed to be enjoying their meal. Sister came in with my wee glass. This time it had about an inch of water.

"Now just sip it very slowly," she repeated and left the ward. I looked around and took a little sip. I'm going to have a little mouthful, I thought. No-one will know. But didn't they! I started to choke. Other patients screamed. Sister ran into the ward, pulled tubes out of my nose and throat, put the oxygen mask on me and sent for the doctors. My wound was bleeding. I had burst the stitches inside of me and all because I didn't do as I was told.

I had to come back ten months later and have an incisional hernia operation. The torn part sewn with steel stitches and I still have it to this day.

*   *   *

In 1973, Mac and I decided to go to Canada to see Dave, Bet, Karen and their new baby girl. She was lovely. They had called her Lydia. We were very impressed. Dave took his holidays while we were there. We went to Penticton. Dave drove us all through the Canadian Rockies. We saw wild bears, bison and antelope. It was lovely. It's a tremendous country. We arrived at Penticton and it was terribly hot. I spent a lot of time in the sea. I can't swim, but Mac can. I floated around and, with his support, I even swam a little. Unfortunately, the little baby became quite ill and had to go into hospital.

After a few days, she began to get a little bit better, so Dave suggested that we take a plane to Calgary to go to see Mac's cousin, Trudy and his aunt and uncle. Then we would go back to Dave's house in Edmonton. This we did. Lena, Charlie and Trudy and her husband made us very welcome. We went to Lena's son's ranch. He breeds race-horses and saw about six of them. We also went to the races to see one of them run, but it didn't win that night. We sat in a private box and had a grand meal while we were watching the racing and I won a few dollars.

After a few days we went back to Dave and Bet's house. Baby was better, so we had the rest of our holiday with them. We did enjoy our first visit to Canada. It was a tremendous success. Dave and his family seemed to be so much nearer now. Whenever, in later years, we paid a visit to Canada, we always paid a visit to Calgary to see Lena, Charley and Trudy. We were always made very welcome. Trudy has been to stay with us a few times also. She and Mac were very fond of each other.

In 1978, the Commonwealth Games were held in Edmonton, Canada, where my youngest son, David, lived with his wife Bet and two daughters, Karen and Lydia. He wrote to us, inviting us to go and said he would get tickets for special events. I wasn't very keen on going. I knew it would be very hot, far too hot for me. Sandra and Mac said that they would love to go.

"Of course you must go," I said, "I know you will enjoy it."

"But what about you, Mum, on your own?"

"Oh! I'll be fine," I reassured them. "Now go and book the plane." All arrangements were made and off they went one evening to get the night train to London. Their plane left Gatwick early the next morning. They were going for three weeks.

I went to bed fairly early for I thought I would give Sandra's bedroom a good clean the next day. She was a very untidy girl, but I always insisted that she had to do her own bedroom. I just left it to her and didn't go near. I bet it's in a mess, I thought as I opened the door, but I didn't expect what met my eyes. On the dressing table was a big sheet of paper propped up.

"Dear Mum,
So that you don't feel too lonely or forgotten, if you follow this piece of string attached to this letter, you will find on the end of it a present, then another for tomorrow and so on, one for everyday we are away. Now don't cheat, just open one each day.
All my love,
San"

I looked. There in a big tea chest were twenty-one beautifully wrapped presents. I just hat to sit on the bed and cry. What a loving kind daughter I had, I wouldn't change her in any way. I didn't cheat. Day after day, I would wake up and think, "I wonder what my present is today?" It did help. It gave me something to look forward to each day.

Mac wrote to me very often and told me all the news of the Games and what they were doing. I was so pleased that they were having such a lovely time. The day they arrived home, I was supposed to be in hospital to undergo tests, but I rang to say I couldn't go until the following day as my husband and daughter would get such a shock on arriving back from holiday to find me in hospital. I went int the next morning and after ten days and lots of horrible tests, I was told that I had diverticolitis. I've learned to cope with this now.

*   *   *

The story I am about to relate is almost unbelievable, but it is absolutely true. My cousin Emmie, who I mentioned earlier, never married. She finally retired to a nursing home in Southport. I would go and visit her about once a month. Her brother, Kenneth, also went to see her now and again. She absolutely adored him. One day, when Mac and I went to see her, Emmie told us that Ken was going to get married to Cathy, who used to be Em's next door neighbour. Kenneth was sixty-five and Cathy, twenty years younger. Em didn't seem too pleased at the idea, but putting her feeloings aside, always made them welcome whenever they went to see her. Ken and Cathy suggested that they would take Mac and I in the car to go and see Em. They lived in a flat near Ormskirk and Mac and I would pay for the lunch. This we were quite agreeable to and it went on for about eighteen months.

One morning, the phone rang. A highly delighted voice from Ken told me that Cathy was pregnant. She hadn't been well and had gone to the doctor. After tests she was proved to be pregnant. They still took us to see Em and they came quite a few times to our home. Mac would go out for a drink with Ken while I would talk to Cathy as I was preparing a meal. She told me that Em had given her power of attorney so that she could sign any of Em's cheques. She said that it would make it easier for Em. Cathy seemed to be getting quite big now and Sandra gave her quite a lot of maternity clothes that she had. One day, after Cathy had been to the doctor's, she rang to say that the doctor thought that she was having twins. After about ten days this was confirmed. They seemed "over the moon". When they were born, Ken would be sixty-seven and Cathy forty-seven.

One day, my sister Lol and her husband, Charley, came to

stay with me for a short holiday. They lived in North Wales. Lol said she would like to go to see Emmie. I rang Ken and he said that we must go to his flat as they had made a nursery and wanted us to see it. Off we went. Well, you should have seen that nursery. It was lovely. Two little white cots with pale pink eiderdowns, a long low white unit containing drawers full of everything a baby could need. The walls were decorated with baby animals. Cathy's friend was there, busy knitting. She said that she thought that she had finished, but now she had to do more for the other twin baby. She had made some lovely things. I took two nightdresses that I had made for Cathy herself.

Time went by. Then, one morning, Ken rang. The babies had arrived. It seems that they were quite small, but had been taken to Alder Hey Children's Hospital. Cathy was fine, but didn't go to the hospital, she wanted to stay at home. It seems that the twins came suddenly. I was elated. I rang the Liverpool Echo and said that my cousin, who was sixty-seven and his wife, who was forty-seven, had just had twin girls. They thought that it was a good story and wondered if they would mind having their picture taken. I said that I'm sure that they wouldn't. They went to Ormskirk, but when Ken opened the door, he wasn't very pleased. They asked if they could go to Alder Hey to take a picture of the babies. Cathy was really mad.

"Don't you dare!" she said. "I'm not having the hospital bothered. They have enough to do. If you go without my permission, I will sue you!" The Echo rang me to tell me what had happened.

"I'm very sorry. It would have been a good story," I said.

Ken and Cathy called at our house every time that they went to see the twins. They were coming on all right, but very slowly.

One day, when they called after their visit to Alder Hey,

Cathy told me that they had thought of moving Em from the nursing home.

"Why?" I asked, "I thought that she was happy there."

"Well,' Cathy replied, "Ken and I noticed that she had bruises on her arms and legs. She said she had fallen. I don't think the nurses are taking care of her the way they should." I was astonished. I always thought how nice the staff were and Em had a lovely room facing the prom and the sea. She always seemed so very happy.

Next week, when Cathy arrived, she was in tears. One of the babies was having breathing problems and they were quite worried about her condition. Five days later, Cathy rang me to tell me the sad news that the baby had died.

"I can't tell you all the details, Marg, I'm too upset." This I understood. I put the phone down.

"Mac, one of the babies has died." I felt so sad. I rang Lol and Sandra and told them the bad news. They were devastated.

On the following Friday, we had not seen nor heard from Cathy or Ken.

"I wonder if they have had the funeral. Give them a ring," Mac said. I phoned and got no answer. "I'll ring tomorrow."

On Saturday, I rang a couple of times and had no reply.

"I can't understand this, Mac," I said. "Perhaps they've gone away for the weekend."

On Sunday, I decided to ring the hospital.

"Could you please give me some information. My cousin had twin baby girls and as they were so small at birth, they were taken to Alder Hey Children's Hospital. One of the babies died on Tuesday and I was wondering how the other one was. I've tried to contact my cousin but can't get any answer when I ring."

"Just a minute. We will find out for you." After a few minutes they came back on the phone.

"I'm very sorry, but we have no twins here. Are you sure you've got the right hospital. I'd try Oxford Street Maternity Hospital. Maybe they can help!" I put the phone down and told Mac. "It's very strange. I can't understand it." I rang Oxford Street. The same reply came.

"Sorry, we can't help, but we've had no twins." I slowly put the phone down. That night, I rang Cathy. She answered the phone.

"Oh Cathy, I've been ringing you all weekend. Where have you been?"

"Oh, Ken and I went away for a couple of days to try to get over our trouble."

"How is the other baby?" I asked.

"She seems to be going on all right."

"Well, Cathy, I rang Alder Hey and they said that they had no twins."

"Oh, she isn't there now," Cathy replied quickly. "I've moved her to Ormskirk Hospital to be nearer home." I was very quiet for a minute. Suddenly, the thought struck me.

"Cathy, you've had no babies have you?" There was a dead silence.

"No," she answered.

"Why? Why have you done this terrible thing?"

"I don't know."

"You have deceived and hoodwinked everybody. I am absolutely disgusted with you both. Ken is just as bad. You have accepted gifts and money from many people. I never, ever want to see either of you again as long as I live." I put the phone down.

The drama didn't end there. That night I lay awake for a

long time pondering on what had happened. Then, suddenly, I remembered about Cathy saying that they were going to remove Emmie from the nursing home. I nearly panicked.

"Mac!" I shouted. He woke up with a start.

"What?"

"They are going to take Em away from the Home and I may never see her again."

"Go to sleep, Marg. We'll talk about this in the morning."

I awoke early. The sun was shining. Over breakfast we discussed what we would do. I rang up the nursing home and asked if the matron would see Mac and I concerning my cousin, Miss Woodcock. After a short wait, I was told that she could see us that day at three o'clock. We caught the train to Southport fairly early to keep the appointment. We were shown into the matron's office and told to take a seat. After a few minutes, she came in. After shaking hands, she sat down.

"Now, what may I do for you?" I started my story.

"Do you know anything about my cousin's brother and his wife?" I asked. She looked at me.

"A little!" was her reply. "Why?" I went through the whole torrid tale.

"We are so concerned about Emmie, in case they take her and we may never see her again." She smiled at me.

"Don't worry, Mrs McDowall. We will never let her go. I am now going to tell you something. We are trying to find them. They have done us out of hundreds of pounds. It is now in the hands of the police. We will take great care of your cousin."

This they did. They were very kind to Emmie, who died twelve months later. Kenneth and Cathy were never found. They had robbed poor Em of all of her money. The council paid for her funeral. I wish we could have afforded to pay, but we hadn't much money. Lol, Charl, Mac and I went to the funeral and took some lovely flowers. One lady from the nursing home was there. She said that they all loved Emmie – as did we all!

During the war, Kenneth who had lived and was born in the same road as I was and with whom I shared my childhood, absconded from the army when he was twenty-one. All the family were very upset. Auntie never heard from him for quite a few years. Then, one day, Auntie got a letter from him to say that he would meet her and Emmie, his sister, in town. Auntie was overjoyed and off they went. They had lunch together, but Ken would not tell them where he was living. As time went by, they often met. Then, one day, Ken told them that he lived in Ainsdale with a woman who was twenty years older than him. She had left her husband for Kenneth. She must have had a bit of money for Ken never went to work. He had no ration book and no national registration card. So, of course, he couldn't apply for a job in case he was found out. Eventually, the Queen granted an amnesty for any deserters from the Army. Kenneth applied and got a free pardon.

He lived with this woman until she was eighty. She became senile and went into a home in Southport to be looked after. Emmie had a small house in Southport. Kenneth was always asking Emmie to help him out with his mortgage etc. Eventually, he had to let the house go. Of course, he had no help money-wise now that his source of income had gone. Em lent him money to set up a small business mending watches, but that soon folded up and Em lost out.

Em's next door neighbour was a nurse at the home where Kenneth's woman friend had gone and that is how Kenneth and Cathy met. They were attracted to each other right away. Em wasn't very pleased as Cathy was married and twenty years younger.

CHAPTER SEVEN

1987–1998

FINAL THOUGHTS

After the war, Lol and Charlie went to live in Birmingham where their son, Paul, was born. They lived there for about four years. Charlie managed to get a good job in Wrexham, North Wales, so they moved once again. I was very pleased at this, for it meant that we could see each other more often. Lol and Charl and Mac and I had some lovely holidays together when the children were grown up. Paul went to university in Cardiff, where he met and married Lynda. They now have three children, Robert, David and Rachael.

As we grew older, Paul wanted his mum and dad to go to Cardiff and live near to where he had bought a very nice house. This Lol did and they bought a lovely bungalow. Lol and Charl spent a lot of their time in the garden, which gave them a whole lot of pleasure. Sadly, after a series of strokes, Charlie's health deteriorated and he died on 2nd January 1995, aged seventy-six.

Sandra took me down to Cardiff for the funeral. Steve stayed home to mind Liam and Lucy. Lucy badly wanted to come with us.

"I like Uncle Charl," she said, but Sandra tried to explain to her little five year old.

"Nanny is on her own now, just like Auntie Lol and, at this time, they just want to be together." After a little pause for reflection Lucy said,

"Well, why don't they go on *Blind Date*." What can one say!

As little boys, Colin and David got on very well together. Dave was a happy-go- lucky child, always smiling. One day, Colin came in crying bitterly. He had a huge red mark on the side of his face.

"Mrs Cass hit me!" he said. "Dave pushed Harold Cass off his bike and Mrs Cass came out and hit me." I saw red. I wasn't a bully in any way, but I ran to Mrs Cass who was standing at her door.

"How dare you hit my son. If my boys want chastising, I will do it and it was Dave who pushed Harold not Colin!" The reason that I was so angry was the fact that she had boxed Colin on the ears and poor Colin had been having such trouble with his ears.

One night, he cried all night with the pain. Next morning, I took him to see the doctor. He told me to lightly syringe his ear with luke warm water. I went to the chemist, bought a syringe and this I did. His other ear started to pain. I went back to the doctor.

"Did you do what I told you to do?"

"Yes, doctor."

"Well, do the other ear also. It will get better." But it got much worse. Colin seemed to be in pain all the time. I was at my wits end. I didn't know what to do.

"Go to see my doctor," Mum said, "in Robson Street, Doctor Baxter. He is very understanding."

Off I went. He looked down Colin's ears.

"Us practitioners don't know enough about any one thing," he said. "I want you to go to the Eye and Ear Hospital where Colin can be seen by a top specialist." I went straight away. After a short wait, we were called into the room where the specialist sat. He looked down Colin's ears. Then he nearly went berserk. He thumped the table with his fists.

"Mother, Mother what have you done?" I told him what the doctor had told me to do.

"Do you know what you have done? You have perforated both ear drums. The water has caused a disease of the inner ear. Nobody, just nobody inexperienced should syringe ears. Who told you to do this?" I told him. He called all the students to take a look.

"Mother," he said, "you will be attending this clinic for the next seven years" and he was right.

Colin has had a very interesting life. He was a very good artist and he painted some wonderful pictures, but as there wasn't much money to be made that way so he had to revert to more commercial activities. He did large murals and became an architect-designer, converting old buildings into modern cinemas and bingo halls. He went to Lybia for six years where he helped to design the new university there and then he returned to London where, like Dave, he opened a restaurant. After a time, while it was still a going concern, he sold the business and bought an old Victorian Coach House in London and converted it into a lovely house.

Marisol become a model. She was very artistic and at one time made her own jewellery and sold it in Harvey Nichols in London. She is now married and lives in Antigua and has a wee boy called Chei.

Jason, like Colin and Dave, was very good with his hands

enjoying carpentry and joinery. Academically he struggled, but at other things he was very good. He now lives in Antigua.

Mac and I had some lovely holidays. We always went with Lol and Charl to Butlin's every year, and really enjoyed the carefree atmosphere there, just doing our own thing. We also went on some smashing tours to Devon and Cornwall – very enjoyable. Mac and I also went to Canada a few more times. Karen, my granddaughter, became a travel consultant and booked us a tour to Las Vegas, San Francisco, San Diego and Los Angeles. We went to Disneyland. It was all so wonderful.

Our last trip to Canada together included a cruise to Alaska, which Karen arranged. We all went, Dave, Bet, Lydia, Karen, Mac and I. The food on board ship was out of this world. There was so much of it. I couldn't eat. They all put on weight, except me. I lost a couple of pounds. The journey was fantastic. We sailed through the North-West Passage, just like Magellan did all those years ago. We went past huge glaciers, saw plenty of whales leaping and having such fun.

When we arrived in Alaska, a small boat met the ship and we were ferried to the mainland. We went to the capital Juno, then to Ketchican and on to Sitka. We went through a lovely old Russian church. It seems unbelievable that Russia sold the whole of Alaska for such a small amount to America.

Mac loved Canada and this was his last visit there. After he died, I didn't think that I would go any more, but twelve months later, Dave and Bet sent me a return ticket to go there for Christmas. They gave me a wonderful time and everybody was so kind. Lydia is a veterinary assistant. She was always very fond of animals. I saw my two great grandchildren, Chelsea and Calin, as well as Dave, Karen's husband. They only live a short distance away from Dave and Bet. Both have lovely homes.

Dave and Bet had a little girl. They called her Karen. She was lovely, with big blue eyes, fair hair and Bet always dressed her like a little princess. On the other hand, Colin and Noli were more way-out and Marisol, who was also very beautiful with her big brown eyes, jet black hair and olive skin, was dressed in tights and long T-shirts.

One day, the two little girls were visiting me. I took them to see a friend of mine, Edna.

"Oh!" she said, "come in! What a beautiful girl you are Karen and what a lovely dress!" Poor Marisol looked down at her T-shirt.

"Mine's pretty too," she said.

"Of course it is dear," Edna quickly replied, "you are two lovely little girls."

"I'll get tea ready now, play nicely together," I said when we arrived back home. Karen came into the back kitchen. "Nanny, 'ave ya got any string?" I looked at her.

"Pardon?"

"'Ave ya got any string?"

"Karen," I said, "Say have, have you got any string." She looked at me with her big blue eyes.

"WANT NO AN! want string!" I had to turn away quickly to hide my smile.

"All right, dear, I'll get your string."

In 1980, my eldest granddaughter, Karen, came to see us from Canada. She had grown into a lovely young lady. She and Sandra had booked to go to Greece for ten days. Just previous to this, Sandra, who was now working at Liverpool University, had met a student there who had asked her for a date. She didn't know whether to go.

"He's younger than me, Mum."

"Well," I said, "it's only a night out. It doesn't mean anything." But it did. The day she got back from Greece, there was a knock on the front door. I opened it. There on the doorstep stood this tall, very good looking young man, carrying a lovely bunch of roses.

"Is Sandra in?" Sandra came into the hall.

"This is Steve, Mum." It developed from there. Steve took her to his home in Hertfordshire to meet his mum and dad, Gwen and George, and two years later they were married.

They now have two children, Liam and Lucy, and live in New Brighton. We see them every weekend and look forward to their visit.

Early in 1991, both Mac and I were quite ill. Social Services very kindly sent me a home help and also arranged "meals on wheels" for us. This was very much appreciated. I slowly began to get better and started to do a bit of my own cooking. So I cancelled the "meals-on-wheels". Mac's progress was much slower than mine, but he seemed to pick up a bit. We played Scrabble and cribbage every day. Our homehelp, Vera, was very nice. She kept the house clean and tidy.

I woke up one morning. It was too early to get up. I lay thinking. I have done nothing with my life. I'm seventy-eight and I have nothing to show for all those years. During breakfast, I broached the subject with Mac.

"Mac, I've done nothing with my life."

"Marg, you've brought up three children, dear."

"I know, but I want to do something else. I'd like to paint." When Colin came down from London the next weekend, Mac told him what I had said.

"Well, Mum, why don't you?"

"Colin, I've never had a lesson."

"That doesn't matter," he said, "as long as you enjoy doing it." He went back to London. The next week a parcel arrived for me. Oil paints and some brushes with a brief letter:

"Now get cracking, Mum! It doesn't matter if it's no good as long as you enjoy doing it. Go to the library and get some books on Art and copy the pictures. That is how you will learn."

This I did. I started off and I loved it. I felt a new life stirring in me. I looked at things in a different way. Mac would watch me.

"Marge, it's wonderful. I didn't know that you could paint."

"No dear, I didn't know either," I replied, but I know now. Day after day, I painted. Mac was so proud.

I know now why God gave me this great gift. He knew he was going to take my dear Mac from me. Six months later he did just that. Steve, my son-in-law, took my darling Mac to Everton to watch a football match and, just before the game started, he collapsed and died. He had had a heart attack. It was a dreadful time. I can't easily put into words how I felt, it goes too deep. I had lost my love, my pal. We had done so much together, been great pals. Even in our retirement, we never got bored with each other. I knew that I would miss him dreadfully.

A couple of months later, I got my paints out. I felt very disgruntled. I looked at the half finished painting I had been doing when Mac had died and decided to finish it. That was the beginning of the comeback. Believe me, it was the best therapy ever. Whenever I feel lonely or sad, I just get my paints out and get lost in another world. I have now done over 100 paintings. My three children are so proud of me. I have been on Granada Television. Colin said that he would like to hold an exhibition of my paintings, but I'm 83 now so I guess that he had better hurry up.

Mac and I saw many wondrous things on our journeys through Canada and America, but some stand out in your memories, never to be forgotten: the opulence of Las Vegas, with its glittering lights; the long Colorado River; the freight trains, which never seem to end; the very tall trees of the Red Forest, some more than 200 feet high; the Athabascan Ice Fields, about 2,000 miles long; beautiful, picturesque Banff; the Crystal Cathedral, all made of glass; sailing through the "North West Passage", with glaciers tall, majestic and powerful; whales leaping and playing in the water, so carefree. We will never forget the Canadian Mounties in their colourful red uniforms and the small village of Solbang, with the Dutch windmills and its small community all dressed in Dutch clothes as worn many years ago. We were privileged to see and to speak to real Indians. We saw totem poles, went through an Indian house on an Indian reservation. It was all very exciting.

One day, while out with Dave, we saw quite a number of people all dressed in black.

"They are Mennonites, Mum," Dave said.

They don't mix with other people. They are self-supporting and grow their own food. They have looms and make their own cloth and clothes and their own implements. They inter-marry, but slowly the race is dying out. They are a very quiet people. No trouble to anyone. If you went to visit their commune, they would be very gracious and welcome you and show you around.

We saw the Canadian Rockies with Bet and Dave. We went to San Francisco and walked along the wharf. We saw Alcatraz, the famous prison in the distance. We went to Disneyland. It was wonderful. We also went to SeaWorld in San Diego. I enjoyed that very much. We have seen so many wonderful things. We have indeed been very privileged.

In 1985, on my eighty-second birthday, I looked back through the years. Sitting in my little terrace house, life was going so very quickly. My three children married and so happy with their families. My eldest son, Colin, had remarried and now has a lovely Japanese wife, Tameia. His two children, Jason and Marisol, are now living in Antigua. I hear from them now and again. I have a home help, Brenda, who is very good doing things in the home that I can't manage myself. I have a lady who does all my shopping, Kate. She is a real gem. My neighbours, Joan, Margaret, Kathie, Lynne and Marie. I can call them all my friends. Other dear friends, Maud and Frank and my dear Primrose and Bob. It makes me feel very humble when I think of all the warmth they bestow on me.

On the walls of my lovely sitting room, I have the pictures that I have copied, my Renoir, my Monet, my Cezanne, my Pissaro, my Sisly, my Gaugin, my Van Gough, my Marisat, my Serrat and my Turner. I have now done over one hundred paintings. I've enjoyed doing them immensely. It has helped me so very much to get over the loss of losing my dear Mac, but I still feel I could do more. I am indeed rich, I **have** done something with my life. I've had a very full and interesting life and so much to thank God for: my eyesight, my clear brain, my hands which can hold this pen so firmly at eighty-three. Something inside me is bursting to get out. I still feel that I can paint some more pictures with God's guidance. I could write. That's it! I could write a book. Tell people all my lovely stories. My life, it's ups and downs, it's laughter and tears. This is not the end, it's the beginning.